The MIDDLE-CLASS NEGRO
in the WHITE MAN'S WORLD

The MIDDLE-CLASS NEGRO in the WHITE MAN'S WORLD

By ELI GINZBERG

with VINCENT BRYAN, GRACE T. HAMILTON, JOHN L. HERMA, *and* ALICE M. YOHALEM

COLUMBIA UNIVERSITY PRESS
New York and London 1967

To LORD SIEFF OF BRIMPTON

NEITHER TIME NOR DISTANCE
CAN WEAKEN THE BONDS OF AFFECTION
OF A QUARTER OF A CENTURY

FOREWORD

In May, 1964, the Field Foundation made a grant to the Conservation of Human Resources Project, Columbia University, to enable it to undertake an exploratory investigation into the career plans of middle-class Negro youth. The Office of Manpower Planning, Evaluation, and Research (OMPER) of the U.S. Department of Labor also contributed to the financing.

The Conservation Project developed an exploratory rather than an experimental design which sought to make two probes—one in Atlanta, the other in New York City—into the career plans of middle-class Negro males currently attending college or college-bound.

We used a case study approach in the hope of developing clues, insights, and new perceptions about how such young Negro men see their broadening opportunities and how they respond to them. Only after such an exploration had been completed could a broad-scale study be designed that would be representative of middle-class Negro youth and would, at the same time, provide a basis for comparisons with white youth. This remains on our research agenda.

This book is devoted to findings from case studies. In

developing the framework within which this investigation was carried out, the Conservation staff drew on its continuing investigations of Negro potential.

The Boards of Education of Atlanta and of New York City and the authorities of Morehouse and Clark Colleges and of City College, Columbia University, and New York University cooperated in this undertaking by enabling us to contact the young men included in the study.

Mrs. Grace T. Hamilton interviewed the Southern contingent and Mr. Vincent Bryan the Northern group. Their initiative and persistence made this study a viable project.

Dr. John L. Herma, my senior collaborator for the last two decades, died just before the final manuscript was completed. He had read and commented on most of the chapters, and had participated actively in the early stages of the work. His death is a source of sorrow to his many friends and co-workers and represents a major loss to social research.

Ruth S. Ginzberg edited the manuscript.

ELI GINZBERG

Director, Conservation
of Human Resources Project

Columbia University
May, 1967

CONTENTS

1: MIDDLE-CLASS YOUTH

Since most Negroes have little opportunity to enjoy the good things of life that are available to the large majority of white Americans, it might be asked why a study should be focused on the Negro middle class. What justification is there for singling out for special concern the fortunate few while neglecting the majority? The answer has several dimensions.

In the first place, there are a great many Negro families, North and South, who are able to take advantage of the broadened educational and occupational opportunities that are now becoming available. Although many Negro men are unemployed, the majority have regular jobs. Although most Negroes who work are concentrated in blue-collar occupations, a significant minority have white-collar jobs. Although a high proportion of Negro families live at the poverty line or below, many have incomes which permit them to live in comfort and security. Although the majority of Negroes do not graduate from high school, a great many do, and there are hundreds of thousands of Negro college graduates. Although family disorganization is widespread among Negroes, most families have the same characteristics as white families—husbands and wives live together and discharge their responsibilities for rearing their children. Although a great many Negroes are needy and oppressed, it is an error to consider all of the 21 million American Negroes in the light of a single poverty prototype.

In the current struggle over Civil Rights, the sympathetic supporter as well as the recalcitrant opponent has tended to stress the negatives in the situation, and this has obscured the existence of the large and growing numbers of Negro families who are no longer poor or ignorant. Such oversimplifications can lead to serious errors in the design and implementation of policies aimed at eliminating segregation and discrimination.

A small number of Negroes have already been able to achieve success in the larger community, but they have been exceptional. The masses of poor and uneducated Negroes are in too weak a position to take ready advantage of the opportunities that are now unfolding. It is the significant number of middle-class Negroes between these two extremes of wealth and poverty who are presently in the most favorable circumstances to respond to the opportunities arising from the racial revolution that is under way.

In the past, Negroes with adequate incomes, educational attainment, and secure family lives were rarely able to enter into the mainstream of American life. Unlike European minorities—the Irish, the Italians, the Jews—Negroes have never become part of the American melting pot. In spite of Gunnar Myrdal's eloquent testimony to the contrary, American democracy, by conviction and commitment, refused to accept the Negro as an equal citizen. The end of legal enslavement did little to change his circumstances. He had been an unwilling slave; he became an unwanted freedman.

While native Americans made assimilation difficult for white newcomers, the passage of time reduced and even eliminated the frictions between the older and newer immigrants. This was a result of the fact that the differences between the European immigrant and the native-born American were primarily cultural, and it required only a generation or so for these differences to fade. Time has not played this role in the assimilation of the Negro, although his forebears arrived in this country as early as the seventeenth century. His enslavement robbed him of his ties to the past. America became his homeland and American traditions became his traditions. Nevertheless, he was kept outside of American society.

While many white immigrants differed from the established population in national origin, religion, language, and customs, the Negroes differed in color—a color that implied savagery, slavery, and stupidity. A black skin persists in a way no foreign accent, no strange religion, no unfamiliar custom does. Furthermore, the antipathy of the whites was institutionalized by law so that there was no way for the black man to merge with the larger white group.

Few Negroes have been able to free themselves of the

disabilities which have followed the various forms of segregation and discrimination that have characterized American society. All Negroes continue to pay a heavy toll because the white community remains color conscious. Those who escaped from poverty and ignorance have been unable to surmount the discrimination and exclusion practiced by the larger society and have been forced to make their way within the Negro community. Regardless of the education they have achieved and their economic circumstances, their plans and their fortunes, as well as those of their children, have been circumscribed by race.

After following a policy of ostracism for three hundred and fifty years, the white community in the United States is beginning to adopt an attitude of tolerance and receptiveness toward the Negro. Intensive efforts are being made to reduce and eliminate racial segregation and discrimination. At long last, America is holding out the promise of equality of opportunity to all citizens.

Equality of opportunity means that individuals can plan for their future without considering the factor of race. In light of America's recent recommitment to this goal, we have sought to determine whether, and to what extent, race continues to play a part in the plans of Negro youths who are otherwise in a position to pursue their goals.

Since significant alterations in the behavior of the American people toward the Negro took place after World War II, particularly after 1954, the best way to judge the response of the Negro community to the slowly but steadily growing receptiveness of the larger society is to focus upon young people who do not carry the full burden of earlier history and practice. We are not concerned here with past wrongs but with future prospects. And the future can be illuminated by centering attention upon a group of young people who are in the process of making their life plans within the structure of the new national receptiveness.

We consider the youths who are the concern of this book to be middle class since they come from families which have some margins of discretion in shaping their lives and in making plans for the future. We are using the concept of "middle class" loosely; we define it for our purposes as a reflection of parental occupations which customarily provide incomes above the poverty level. Occupationally, the parents range from lower middle-class service workers to upper middle-class professionals. Since our primary interest was the aspirations of Negro boys who do not have to contend with poverty and who can look forward to parental help in realizing their educational and occupational goals, this definition appears reasonable. We sought youths whose family circumstances permitted them some scope of choice. Other criteria of social status could not be determined at the time of selecting young men for interviewing but we subsequently discovered that the families of the youths selected had additional characteristics associated with the middle class.

Shortly after the turn of the century, when W. E. B. DuBois wrote his incisive analysis of the Negro community, *The Souls of Black Folk*, he dealt at length with the "talented tenth"—that thin crust of leadership among Negroes who, despite tremendous obstacles, had raised themselves out of deep poverty and ignorance. Franklin Frazier, writing a half century later, dealt with a successful group that was only slightly larger. Our broader definition of the Negro middle class includes roughly one-third of the 21 million American Negroes—those who have incomes above the poverty level, stability of employment, and reasonable opportunities for education. It is this much-expanded base that lends substance to contemporary discussions about whether the future of the Negro in the United States is to be conceived in terms of the characteristic model of ethnic minorities who, originally despised and harassed, were able, nevertheless, to fight their way into American society.

Since we knew from our earlier study, *Occupational Choice: An Approach to a General Theory* (1951), that occupational planning is a process that takes place over a considerable number of years and that young people are able to adopt a realistic attitude toward their alternatives only as they reach late adolescence, we decided to include three groups: high-school seniors, college sophomores, and college seniors. These three groups cover, for the most part, an age range from seventeen to twenty-two, although some boys were younger and a few were older. By concentrating on these three grade levels, we were able to study young people at different levels maturity as they confronted decisions about their future.

Although college attendance itself can confer middle-class status upon students from lower-class backgrounds, these young people can achieve a higher education only through exceptional effort, often with considerable personal sacrifice. Since we sought to assess the effect of race on aspirations, we selected students whose college orientation was more likely to be a consequence of middle-class expectations and whose families could provide them with support and encouragement.

Our primary aim was to examine the perceptions of a group of middle-class Negro college youth of the reality they confront and their responses to it. We hoped to learn how they see their future and what they are trying to do to shape it according to their hopes and desires. In this way, we should gain insight into whether the integration of the Negro into American society is likely to follow the pattern of other minorities or whether it will remain unique.

2: THE STUDENTS

In order to learn how Negroes are responding to the new career opportunities that are being opened to them, we decided to concentrate on men, since many fields are discriminatory with respect to sex as well as to race. If we had included women in our study, we would not have been able to delineate as sharply the ways in which employment opportunities are being broadened through the removal of racial barriers. Moreover, the career planning of women is heavily conditioned by considerations of marriage and children, and this would have made it difficult to assess the impact of changes specifically related to race.

Negro college men from middle-class homes represent a sizable group. The traditional approach to the analysis of such a group is to develop a representative national sample of several thousand and then systematically to interview them or ask them to complete a questionnaire. There is much to be said for both of these conventional approaches, but we proceeded differently.

Cost was one reason to seek an alternative approach, but it was only one. It seemed wise to structure our inquiry so that a relatively small number of young men could be interviewed at considerable length in order to follow the ramifications of their thinking. We knew, from our earlier research, that the processes of educational and occupational choice are subtle and complex and that a brief interview or limited questionnaire would not adequately reveal the decision-making of the adolescent or young adult.

We therefore decided to limit the size of the group to permit interviews in greater depth. We were aware of the advantages of an approach predicated on a representative sample but we concluded that such a study might well be postponed until a more modest effort had been carried through and its lessons extracted.

Although we did not intend to conduct a broad national study, we did include young men from two different regions—North and South. Since most Negroes are urban, we selected Atlanta and New York as our two centers of investigation, not because they are typical but because each has a large concentration of the Negro middle class as well as large numbers of Negro college students.

The principal reason for selecting both a Northern and a Southern component was to take account of differences in regional environment and of reactions of young people to these differences. We did not know at the outset of our investigation whether regional differences would be significant, but we wanted to be sensitive to any that might exist.

We decided to interview 20 young men in each city at

each of the three educational levels—high-school seniors, college sophomores, and college seniors—a total of 120.

Because of the exploratory nature of our study, we decided to use an open-ended interview through which we would seek to capture in the respondents' own words how they appraised the present and the future and the plans that they were making to realize their goals. To assure that the interviews were comparable, we developed a list of subjects to be covered. With these as a guide, the interviewers were able to elicit additional information when the respondents' first answers did not seem to reflect adequately their thinking and planning.

No one who has had experience in interviewing will question the hypothesis that unless the interviewer gains the confidence of the respondent, the effort will be constricted and unsatisfactory. In light of today's highly charged racial atmosphere, it seemed essential to assign Negro staff members as interviewers to reduce this hazard.

The interviews in New York City were conducted by a male who is engaged in the private practice of psychotherapy. Our staff member in Atlanta is a woman who has had many years of experience in community work and who was elected to the Georgia state legislature while this study was in progress.

Through the cooperation of the Boards of Education in Atlanta and New York City we obtained access to high schools located in middle-class residential areas and attended by considerable numbers of Negroes who were college-bound. We were permitted to study the registration records of Negro students in order to select a sufficient number who met our requirement that a parent be engaged in white-collar employment. In addition, where the information was available, we selected boys who had at least one parent who had completed high school. Through these simple criteria we were able to rule out youths who came from families in such straitened economic and social conditions that their career aspirations and planning were restricted.

Morehouse College was the source of the majority of the Atlanta college component, and Clark College provided the remainder. Both are private Negro institutions. In New York City, the group was chosen from among three institutions: the College of the City of New York, the Washington Square College of New York University, and Columbia College. The first institution is public, and about half of the Northern group were New York residents enrolled there as tuition-free day students. The other colleges are privately endowed and charge high tuition.

Since the Southern colleges enroll Negro students almost exclusively, the interviewer had only to scan registration information to select students with the appropriate background. In the Northern integrated institutions, however, the interviewer was confronted with two hurdles. The first was to make contact with Negro students. The second was to determine whether they met our middle-class criterion. Since the college records in New

York City do not carry racial designations, we were not able to obtain a list of prospective interviewees. Rather, we were forced to rely on indirect approaches—making contact through helpful faculty and students, and using direct approaches at student centers. These informal contacts sometimes resulted in interviews which subsequently had to be discarded because the respondents did not meet our requirements. Additional interviews were substituted.

The absence of racial identification on personnel records points up one of the paradoxes of the Civil Rights movement. For many years, racial data were used to the disadvantage of Negroes and the Negro leadership was successful in interdicting their use. However, without this information, it has become very difficult, in many areas, to exert leverage against employers and officials to provide broadened opportunities for minorities. For example, it would surely be desirable, particularly in educational institutions wholly or partially supported by government, to know the characteristics of the student body in order to determine the degree of racial integration.

There were important differences between the Northern and Southern institutions represented in our study. Interviews were conducted in one Northern high school which was racially integrated and in two Atlanta high schools which were still segregated. We do not know to what extent these Southern schools are handicapped by their segregated faculties and student bodies, but we may conjecture that, like most segregated Negro schools, these high schools suffer from relative inadequacies, particularly in the areas of teacher training and student preparation.

The three Northern colleges are superior to the two Negro institutions in faculty, student body, and physical resources. Although Morehouse, in particular, is a Negro institution of the highest repute, it is still handicapped in its attempt to provide an education equal in scope and quality to that available in these Northern integrated colleges.

However, once we had decided to use two different regional environments, we had no option but to include institutions of varying strengths since any study of the Negro college student must include those who attend Southern Negro institutions which continue to serve over 60 percent of the Negro college population.

There are two principal ways of making use of interview materials. One is to extract the information furnished by the respondents and to organize it into statistical categories for systematic analysis and evaluation. To proceed in this manner requires more control over sampling, more cases, and more systematic interviewing than we considered necessary or desirable. Therefore, we do not present any tables and we have limited our use of data to suggesting orders of magnitude.

We have taken an alternative case-study approach in exploiting the interview materials. We have grouped the responses around a series of major themes, organizing the statements made by the respondents about the major points of interest and concern to them. By quoting liberally from these interviews we have sought to capture and retain their freshness and directness. We have made a deliberate attempt to bring the youths and the reader into direct contact. We have sought to differentiate between what the young men told us and our interpretation of what they said, so that the reader is given an opportunity to make his own assessment.

Because the heart of this book derives from materials elicited from these open-ended interviews, we will illuminate the interviewing process by calling attention to some of the reactions of both the interviewees and the interviewers.

The importance of rapport between interviewer and interviewee is suggested by the following quotation from the interview of a Northern college senior: "I think I spoke more truthfully to you than I have on any previous occasion. Your questions have already caused me to ask myself some more." Another Northern senior stated: "I liked the interview. It gave me an opportunity to give you my capsule views on things that have real significance. I found it more stimulating than most interviews."

The last comment indicates that being interviewed was not a strange or new experience for some. A blasé attitude toward being interviewed was expressed by another Northern college senior who said: "I'm used to being interviewed—you didn't bother me." Another student admitted that at first he had been reluctant to talk with anyone because of previous experiences with "deceitful college officials. But I'm glad I came. I was able to organize my thoughts in a more meaningful way."

Remarks which indicated that students had gained clarification about their career plans from the interview were made time and again. A Northern high-school student commented: "I had never before made a comparison of my life with my father's or vice versa, and that gives me something to think about." A Southern college sophomore said: "I've enjoyed the talk. Since I've been at Morehouse I have met only two teachers who seemed interested in trying to help students with their problems."

A Southern high-school senior remarked: "I am quite flattered to be asked for this interview." But another was skeptical: "Why is this so important and what use will it be put to? Explain to me why people want to know what I think." The same kind of reaction was exhibited by another Southern high-school lad who blurted out: "This is my first interview. I was shocked. At first, I thought it was for a job. Are all students being interviewed? Am I the only one? What is the type of student that is being interviewed?"

Our previous experiences in interviewing adolescents and young adults had demonstrated that a discussion of future plans is likely to be considered by many as an opportunity for clarification. And this is exactly how several boys reacted. A Northern college sophomore: "Some of your questions touched on things I've been thinking about which I have never brought out in the open before. Some things I never thought seriously about in a conscious way." A high-school senior, also from the North, said: "It certainly brought out my thoughts on things and how I feel; and it brought out the point that I had better think about my future more."

Because of their strategic role in the study, the reader may be interested in a few of the comments the interviewers appended. Talking of a Columbia senior, our Northern interviewer commented: "This young man accepts, as a matter of course, the responsibility for achieving at a high level, just as if this is the only appropriate action to take." About another college senior, he said: "He is the only student who pointed out the socio-cultural role of Negro students in exposing whites to more realistic images of Negroes." About still another senior, he said: "H.B. was impressive, his delivery and stance during the interview were unmistakably mature, and his point of view regarding Negroes suggests a deep and genuine identity between his self and Negroes as a class. This is not always so clearly projected by interviewees."

Our Southern staff member had the following to say about some of her interviewees. A Morehouse senior: "Extremely polite and I gathered a bit sensitive about setting forth his ideas on how prejudice has affected him in his personal life." A sophomore: "He did not talk easily. I couldn't be sure whether he was thinking over real answers to questions or considering what was acceptable to say." About another college sophomore: "He seemed to me a typical example of a youth in a stable, rising, middle-class family."

Our interviews aimed to bring one dimension of the problem of race relations into focus: how middle-class Negro youth are responding to their new opportunities. In selecting this point of departure we have made two explicit commitments: we believe that the findings are important in their own right since they are derived from representatives of a significant minority of Negroes; and we are concerned with whether and to what extent the discoveries about these middle-class youngsters have applicability to the rest of the Negro population. By tracing their family backgrounds, education, and aspirations, we should be better able to assess their prospects of making their way in a white man's world and to gain some indication of the prospects of other young Negroes.

3: HEADSTART

There has been unresolved conflict in American life between our long-standing commitment to the doctrine of equality of opportunity and the fact that children from different families have different life chances. Possibly the most strategic social circumstance affecting a child's future prospects is the home into which he is born. By selecting members of the middle class as subjects for this study we were deliberately excluding youths from families whose lack of occupational attainment would handicap their children's prospects of achievement.

Our criterion for middle-class status was minimal—white-collar employment assuring an income above the poverty level. Although the families of a few of the young men barely met this qualification, many had parents at a considerably higher level. As we shall now demonstrate, the environments in which these boys were reared were, as hypothesized, conducive to the development of high educational and career aspirations.

The average level of schooling attained by the fathers of our group is somewhere between high-school and college graduation, that is, college attendance for less than four years. However, three-quarters of the Southern group have fathers who acquired at least a Bachelor's degree, in contrast to only about 20 percent of the Northerners. Of 11 fathers who had earned doctorates, primarily in medicine or dentistry, 8 are Southerners. There are 4 Ph.D's, 2 each in the North and South. There are 9 men, 7 of them fathers of Northern boys, who have less than a high-school education. The extent to which the fathers of our interviewees had achieved a level of educational attainment above that of most Negro males in the same age groups is revealed by the 1960 Census which shows an average level of schooling of about seven years. As a matter of fact, the median level for white males was not quite ten years of schooling.

The education of the mothers of our group is very similar to that of the fathers; they have the same average number of years in school, at some point within college. Over three-quarters of the mothers in the South acquired a minimum of a Bachelor's degree. This was true for somewhat over a fifth of the Northern mothers. There are 3 of the mothers who have Ph.D.'s and 15 who have obtained Master's degrees, primarily in the fields of education or social work. At the lowest end of the scale, 4 mothers, all Northerners, had not gone beyond elementary school. Our group is much more highly educated than the average Negro woman of comparable age who has completed eight years of school and the average white woman who attended school for ten and a half years.

Further understanding of the family backgrounds of our young men can be obtained by comparing the levels of education achieved by their fathers and those achieved by their mothers. The group divides more or less equally into three patterns: fathers who have more education than mothers, parents who have had the same level of education, and mothers who have had more education than fathers. All but 4 of the 37 Southern fathers who are college graduates married women who had graduated from college. In the North, this is true of less than half of the male college graduates. In the two-thirds of the families where there are differences in the level of educational achievement of the spouses, the extent of the difference is rather narrow, such as a high-school graduate married to a person with some college, or a high-school graduate married to a college graduate.

The college and professional schools that the majority of parents attended were Southern Negro institutions, regardless of the region in which they presently reside. In a few instances, interviewees reported that their mothers are currently students in college or graduate school. A Southern student said: "My mother is thirty-six; she finishes college and I finish high school this year." A Northern high-school senior reported: "My father graduated from high school and attended Cooper Union but did not get a degree. My mother is a college graduate and is now attending Hunter College for her Master's degree in social work." A Southern college student said: "My mother attended Prairie View College and is now working on a Master's degree at North Texas State University which was recently integrated."

The relatively high level of education that their parents had achieved suggests that the young men in our study grew up in homes where learning was respected and where strong pressures were exerted on them to go to college. However, the likelihood of their going to college depended not only on their parents' educational background but also on their ability to finance higher education. Generally, the level of education achieved has a direct influence upon occupational level, but this has not been as true for Negroes as it has for whites, since restrictions due to racial discrimination have sharply limited the access of educated Negroes to many fields within their competence. Thus, many Negroes of high educational attainment are able to stimulate their children intellectually but are unable to provide the financial support for intellectual endeavors.

This was not true for most of the fathers of these young men, however, for they appear to be in occupations that reflect their educational achievements. Over half of the fathers are found in professional or managerial occupations, that is, self-employed or salaried in such fields as medicine, law, accounting, the ministry, teaching, undertaking, and construction. The second largest group are in sales or clerical occupations: auditors, postal clerks, IBM processors, etc. Service and blue-collar occupations account for a quarter; the former are men engaged in such occupations as policemen, truck drivers, guards, building superintendents; the blue-collar workers include mechanics, carpenters, bricklayers, and seamen. Sons of blue-collar workers were included if their mothers are engaged in white-collar employment. The favorable occupational distribution of these fathers is evident when one compares them with all Negro men, less than 5 percent of whom are in professional and managerial occupations. Even if we compare our group with white males, we find the gross comparison favors these Negro men; only about one-quarter of all white males are in the two top occupational categories.

The occupational level of our Southern fathers is noticeably higher than the Northern group. About 3 out of 4 Southern men are in the professional or managerial categories, while only a third of the Northerners are.

This is how some of the young men described their fathers' work. A Southern high-school student said: "My father is now a general practitioner and surgeon. He is a member of the Fulton County Medical Association and American Medical Association. He is on the Board of Trustees of Morris Brown College. He's also on the Board of the Citizens' Trust Company."

Another had a father who holds two jobs: "My father came back from World War II and is a plasterer for the Board of Education. He is also a minister of the First Baptist Church in Athens, Georgia."

The same picture of dual jobs is reflected in the following: "My father is a licensed electrician. He has a shop in his basement. He works on air conditioners, and on TV's and on IBM machines and other machines like that. He is also employed at the post office. He is a zip code specialist in the dead letter department."

A Northern high-school interviewee told us: "My father is head timekeeper at the Brooklyn Navy Yard. He is under tension right now on account of the Navy Yard closing."

We also were interested in whether the boys' mothers work outside the home. Since World War II there have been two trends in women's participation in the world of work. More and more educated married women from middle-class families have entered or reentered the labor force to work part or full time. In addition, as incomes have risen, a smaller percentage of less educated married women whose husbands are at the lower end of the occupational scale have found it necessary to go to work to supplement the family's resources.

Historically, a much higher proportion of Negro women have worked than have white women as a result of the much lower levels of family income characteristic of the Negro population, regardless of social class. While more Negro than white women continue to work, the gap is narrowing. One reason for this is that the educated white woman is joining her Negro counterpart in the labor market. While women from lower-income homes tend to work out of necessity, those from middle-class homes frequently do so out of preference.

In our group, 3 out of 4 of the mothers are employed. Only 1 in 4 can be classified as a housewife. A higher proportion of the mothers of these boys work than the national average; the comparable figure for all Negro mothers in this age group is 44 percent; for all white mothers it is 36 percent.

A second finding of significance is that over two-thirds of the women who work are in professional or technical positions, primarily school teachers. The next largest concentration of employed mothers is in clerical occupations; the remainder are factory operatives or in personal service occupations. Reflecting the marked differences in their educational achievement, only 1 Southern woman is employed as a domestic servant and none as a factory worker, while in the North, 12 are so employed. The husbands of these women work at white-collar jobs.

The most striking finding of all perhaps is the fact that of the 53 women with at least a Bachelor's degree, no fewer than 50 are currently employed. This very high ratio is one additional piece of evidence in support of the now increasingly clear trend that the more education a woman has, the more likely she is to work.

Here are a few sons' descriptions of their mothers' work:

"My mother taught at North Carolina College and is now at Atlanta University where she teaches educational psychology; she also teaches gifted and mentally retarded children, that is, exceptional children."

"My mother is presently employed by the Henrietta Abelson Hospital for Children. She is a registered nurse."

"My mother is a substitute teacher in Nashville and is working toward a Master's degree in Education at A & I College."

"My mother teaches as a home demonstration agent. She teaches parents to sew. And she teaches handicapped people to adjust to their environment."

All of these quotations were made by young men living in the South. The Northerners did not go into as much detail, but we learned some of the positions held by their mothers: cashier in a supermarket, machine operator in a dress factory, supervisor in the Welfare Department.

Approximately 1 out of 4 mothers do not work but keep house for their husbands and care for their children. It should be emphasized that there are twice as many housewives in the North as in the South, probably reflecting, in the first instance, their lower level of education in conjunction with their husband's ability to support them and, in the second instance, the lower incomes in the South despite a generally higher occupational status. The wives of Northern professionals are more likely to be homemakers than are the wives of Southern professionals, although in both cases they represent a minority of such wives. In fact, in no husbands' occupational group are more wives at home than at work. The highest proportion of homemakers is found among the wives of service employees, about half of whom are home. The smallest number of homemakers are among the wives of managers and proprietors, only one of whom is home.

A comparison was made between the occupational levels of husbands and wives, generally based on skill and educational requirements of their fields of work. In approximately 40 percent of the families, the fathers have a higher occupational status than their wives; in about 33 percent there is a basic equality; and in the remaining 27 percent, the wives have better jobs. The point to note is that in approximately 3 out of 4 families the man's work status is superior to or equal to that of his wife's. This is congruent with the conventional pattern in middle-class white America.

Illustrations of situations in which women hold the more prestigious job are the following. In the South, the man is a building superintendent, his wife a teacher of speech; another man is a janitor, his wife is a high-school teacher. In the North, we have a man who is a guard at a housing development, while his wife is a registered nurse; in another instance a man is a patrolman for the Transit Authority, his wife, a junior high-school teacher. But these inversions are relatively infrequent and the spread is not usually very great.

Now that we have described their parents' educational and occupational attainments, we shall discuss the type of family structure within which these youths have been reared. The vast majority of them come from normal families; 4 out of 5 are living with both natural parents. The remainder either have one stepparent or are living with their mothers who have been widowed, divorced, or separated. Because of the widespread exaggerations about the instability of Negro family life, it should be emphasized that only four of the families in our study are headed by mothers who have been divorced or separated from their husbands. This low number of broken families supports the position of those who contend that Negro family instability is more likely to be related to economic disability than to racial peculiarities.

A further indication of the middle-class identity of this group is that most of the young men come from small families. About half come from families with only one or two children. There are only nine families with more than five children—one with ten, two with seven, and six with six children. There is no significant difference in family size between the Northerners and Southerners.

Additional understanding of their family circumstances can be gained through an examination of the educational achievements and occupational status of the older siblings in these families. We have educational information about most of the eighty-one older siblings, forty-seven of whom are sisters. Over three-quarters of the older brothers of our Southern group have had some college experience; 40 percent of these are currently attending college or have already graduated; the remainder have dropped out. There are no college graduates among the older brothers of our Northern group, but almost half of them have had some college and one older brother is now a college student. None of the brothers,

North or South, who are college graduates has gone on to graduate school as yet.

In the South, every older sister who has completed her education has at least a college degree. The others are presently college students. Four of the college graduates have received Master's degrees and one has her M.D. In the North, most older sisters have not gone beyond high-school graduation; seven sisters have either left college or are now in college. There are two college graduates, both of whom have acquired Master's degrees.

Another way of looking at the educational achievement of older siblings is to disregard sex and to consider the highest level reached by any older offspring in a family. We have data about forty-six families. We find that in half of these families a sibling who is old enough to have completed college has acquired at least a Bachelor's degree. There is no family in which at least one older child has not completed high school and this relatively low level of achievement is characteristic of less than one out of five families. Among the twenty-four Southern families, there are only three in which at least one older offspring has not acquired a college degree or is not presently studying for one.

Thus, we see that many of the boys in our sample are not innovators in seeking a college education, but are following a family pattern. This is particularly true in the South where the college goals of those who have older siblings reflect the experiences of their parents and of at least one older brother or sister, and the goals of most of those without older siblings are inspired by parental models. In the South, this generation, with its large number of college graduates and college students who are likely to graduate, is attaining a level of education at least equal to its parents; and in the North, where parents and older siblings are less likely to have been college graduates, it will far excel its family's achievements.

The occupational status of older siblings also affords an indication of family status. Fifty older brothers and sisters are either in the labor force, in the armed services, or are housewives. Five sisters are homemakers. Of the remaining forty-five, about a third are in the top occupational grouping, professional or managerial, and slightly under a quarter are in sales and clerical positions. Somewhat over a quarter of the group are in lower level occupations, blue collar and service, and the remainder are in the armed forces.

In most of these cases, occupational status is a reflection of educational achievement. Thus, Southern siblings tend to be more strongly represented in high level jobs than the Northerners. However, there is some indication that a few siblings have jobs that are not commensurate with level of education achieved; this is presumably a result of racial discrimination. For example, a young woman with a B.A. is working as a receptionist, one with two years of college is working as a nurse's aide, and a young man with some college is working as a terminal starter.

This is how members of our Southern group talked about their siblings:

"I have three brothers, no sisters. One brother married at 27. He spent three years in college at Prairie View and is married. He is an assistant clerk at a bank. Another brother who did not go to college is at home. He is a laborer, a truck driver. You see, he tried to wait on the oldest brother and wanted to finish school and go to college with him."

"My older sister was born in New Orleans. She's pretty nice. She's a very kind person and ambitious. She's relatively considerate towards the family. She has a B.S. from Spelman. She went to Atlanta University and took chemistry and then to Xavier and got her degree in pharmacy. She taught one year at Bennett College. She is presently employed by the Triangle Prescription shop. My next sister has an A.B. degree from Spelman. She is good in art and music. She studied at Colorado State University. She doesn't have an M.A. She is an elementary school teacher. Sister Ruth, who is closest to me, had a B.S. from Spelman. She went to Ohio State for two years, then to Indiana for one year, then to Meharry for four years. She did her residency at a New York City hospital and her internship was spent mostly at Knickerbocker Hospital in New York. I believe she did her residency at Bellevue Hospital. The next year she went to New York University to get another degree in psychiatry and now she is doing a residency in psychiatry and neurology. I have been influenced by my sisters to go into a science."

"I have two older sisters, one is at Bennett and the other at the University of Pennsylvania. I'm not the smartest one in the family. It seems as though I came after the smart ones, so I had it rough, but I made out O.K. Around here I have to do all the heavy work. I get no special attention."

"I expect to help my sister through college. She wants to be a lab technician and she has promised to help me through medical school."

Among the older siblings of our Northern group are the following: the son of an air conditioning salesman, who is currently a sophomore at New York University, reports that he has an older brother who is a junior at City College and a younger sister still in elementary school. Another New York University sophomore reports that his oldest sister is a senior at Brooklyn College preparing to teach; another older sister is a sophomore at City College; two of his younger brothers are attending high school; and his youngest sister is still in junior high school.

A college senior who has six older siblings told us that two of his older sisters are housewives and the third is a practical nurse. All finished high school. One of his older brothers is a hospital aide with two years of college, another is a civil service clerk, and the third is a construction contractor. These last two are high-school graduates.

A City College senior, aged twenty, whose father, a music teacher, is a graduate of Julliard and whose mother, a college graduate, is a registered nurse, has an older sister who is a college freshman and a younger sister who attends parochial school.

A dimension of the environment in which these young men grew up is revealed by the contrast between their parents' background and their own. The following excerpts from interviews of Southern boys emphasize the difficult paths that some of their fathers had to tread:

"My father was born in south Georgia. He was reared in Tuskegee because his parents moved there when the white people in their home town would not provide a school. My grandfather had a farm and was a minister."

"My father was born in Tennessee and moved to Mississippi when he was four. He was brought up by a poor father and finished Morehouse by working on a tobacco farm in Connecticut in the summers to pay his tuition."

"In my father's family there were seven boys and one girl and my father was about the only one who made good. He worked very hard and made a lot of progress."

There were others whose fathers were more fortunate:

"Father was in the service in 1955, in the Air Force Reserve, and he was the only colored man who had a good job. He was a Master Sergeant at the Dobbin Air Field."

"I am a great-grandson of a retired president of West Virginia State College."

Here is what some of our Northern interviewees reported:

"My father lived in south Jamaica (Queens) and attended Jamaica High School. Higher education was not stressed then and his main educational goal was to get out of high school."

"My father wasted his talents. He's a brilliant musician. He did the easiest thing. He sat behind a piano and taught students."

"My father had to stop school in junior high school to support his family. His mother had left home and he was raised by his grandmother—the grandfather had left too. He could not take advantage of higher education. A profession for him was always out of the question."

"My grandfather was well off and there weren't many problems. My father came from a family of musicians."

It appears that a large number, if not the majority, of fathers have achieved middle-class status by dint of their own efforts, but there are others who were born into the middle class. As a matter of fact, there are several indications, such as reports of long-time family connections with certain colleges, that some of these boys are members of families whose middle-class status had been acquired long ago. Although their parents and grandparents and even some great-grandparents had to function exclusively within the Negro community, in that milieu they were able to acquire the social and economic characteristics of the middle class.

In addition to commenting on their parents' backgrounds, a few boys touched on their own lives within their families.

A Southern sophomore said: "My family is a very

close family and we love one another and like to be together. We play cards together and we play games together and we have music sessions together. I would like this type of close-knit family life for my children."

The key role of the father is underlined in the following two cases. "I discuss all my plans every minute with my father. If he gives me advice he always tells me he will help me do what I want to do. He has never refused me. Oh, we are close, as close as can be. I told him I didn't want him to help me. I tell him all of my plans."

"My relationship with my father is close. I love my father. He is trying to get up money for my school. Next year I am going to Howard University. I admire the whole family. I am proud of my mother. She has get-up-and-go. We scrap but I love her. My sister is visually handicapped. She is in the eighth grade. She sings. We are quite close. She is remarkable. She also has get-up-and-go. The general relationship of the family is close. Although they don't show it, every member of the family loves each other."

We have intertwined the foregoing materials about the lives and experiences of these boys' parents and siblings to consider, at least briefly, the role of the family in preparing young people for work and life. While some individuals can leap over major hurdles and make their way without a helping hand from their parents, this is a comparatively rare occurrence. The vast majority of young people are strongly influenced by their parents and the kinds of upbringing they provide.

Most white Americans are born and raised in families

which can provide their children with a reasonable start in life. Belonging to the white majority rather than to a minority without status, they are likely to ignore or minimize the hurdle of race in the career and life planning of Negroes. Among the important factors of which they are likely to have no awareness or sensitivity is the personal insecurity that has for so long attached to a Negro's everyday life. What growing up and living in an environment characterized by antagonism and oppression does to children and adults can be fully appreciated only by those who have been directly exposed to such conditions.

It is also difficult for the white majority to appreciate fully the serious inadequacy of the educational opportunities available to Negroes. Most white people themselves have only recently become more fully aware of the importance of a good education as a prerequisite for getting a good job and leading a good life, and few among them really understand that de jure and de facto segregation have forced most Negroes to attend inferior schools.

Since their access to opportunity has been greatly restricted because of their color, Negro children, even more than white children, have been affected by the position of their parents. The jobs which their fathers and mothers hold, the total family income, the neighborhood in which they reside, have been even more influential for Negroes than for whites because racial barriers severely limit opportunities for upward mobility.

Despite the tremendous costs of segregation, it has

had some minor compensations for some Negroes. For instance, there have been a series of jobs, from physician and minister to teacher and undertaker, that are reserved within the Negro community for Negroes. Hence, a small minority have had an opportunity to rise occupationally and economically.

But we should quickly put this advantage into perspective. The same system of segregation was responsible for the fact that until after World War II, no Negro had access to a school of engineering in the South although, except for teachers, engineers represent the single largest group of male professionals. Nor should we overlook the fact that very few Negroes become businessmen, in large measure, because of the inability of Negroes to secure credit. These limitations apply to the North as well as the South, but they have been more oppressive in the South because this region has contained the substantial majority of Negroes.

Nevertheless, although segregation had a legal basis in the South, it was deeply entrenched in the North. There, too, Negroes had access primarily to second-rate schools and third-rate jobs—not by law, but by tradition and informal restrictions. There may have been less stigma to being a Negro in the North, but, that said, we must quickly add that Northern Negroes have still been second-class citizens, like their Southern brothers.

The young men in our study, living in a time when the negatives of color are beginning to recede, appreciate that their chances to make something of themselves in this world have been greatly affected by what their parents have been able to achieve. For they can start off at the point at which their parents have arrived.

We have seen some contrasts between the nature of their fathers' lives and their own. This is how they see the contrast between their fathers' opportunities at their age, and what they now see for themselves. A Northern college senior noted: "My father knew what hunger was. This has not been true for me." A Northern high-school senior described his father's background: "He did not have it as easy as I did. He came from a poor family. There were four children. He grew up in Harlem during the depression and things were pretty rough. His mother died when he was young. At seventeen, he wasn't going to school; he was working. By comparison, I am coming up in a period of prosperity. There are jobs available, educational opportunities and you can plan for a career." A Northern sophomore said: "Opportunities are greater for me. My father was born in the South and had family obligations which limited his aspirations and mobility. My horizons are greater and it will be easier for me to achieve."

Better access to education was noted by a great many of the youths. Most of them ascribe this largely to improved finances. "I guess the basic difference is money," said a Northern sophomore, "and the opportunity to go to college. My father had to go to work and I didn't have to. There are more advantages now for Negro young men. Males didn't go to college then as now." A senior at CCNY remarked: "I have much more since I live in the North and my father's youth was spent in the South. My father never had before him anything like a city university or the promise of a first-class education. At twenty-one, he was working. At twenty-one, I'm studying for a degree."

A Southern college senior, talking about his opportunities, said: "It will be much easier. In my father's day it was difficult for Negroes to get an education. They had to scrape up the finances to go to graduate school. They had to help other members of the family. The families were larger. My family is smaller and my parents can see me through Morehouse." A Southern sophomore said: "My father worked his way through college. I think it will be easier for me—financially, I would be willing to work to shoulder some of the expenses, but I don't think I'll have that problem. There are so many fellowships and assistantships available."

Broadening opportunities for Negroes in general have additional dimensions. One boy mentioned that "just getting a letter from Harvard in response to an appliction for enrollment is an achievement which would not have occurred twenty-five years ago."

A dentist's son who is a senior in a New York high school and who has been accepted at Amherst reported that his father "could not get into the school for which he was qualified. He had to pick the second best dental school. If he had my opportunities, he would be much further than he is now."

Some students stressed that there had been a change in attitude toward education which redounded in their favor. A Northern sophomore said about his patrolman father who attended a New York high school: "Higher education was not stressed then and his main educational goal was to get out of high school. This limited his horizons as to education and job opportunities and also social environment. None of this is applicable to me."

Educational opportunity is one side of the coin; career opportunity, the other. "There are potential career opportunities available to me that my father never had," said a Northern college senior. A Northern sophomore, the son of a mechanic, remarked: "I'll end up with a career, whereas my father ended up with a job."

Along the same lines, a Southern college senior stated: "In my parent's day, discrimination was at its peak. Negroes never thought about applying for certain positions." A classmate agrees that "jobs were not as open in my parents' generation. Instead, there was no choice except to teach or to try for small business." A Northern sophomore said: "I have more job opportunities available to me. Things are better for me. I can achieve if I wish to." A Southern sophomore remarked: "My father could consider work opportunities only within the Negro world, but this is no longer necessary."

With better educational and career opportunities, our young Negro men look forward to earning more and living better than their parents. A Southern college senior expects to start with a higher salary than his father did: "I would be better off seeing as how a Negro preacher did start off as a ball of fire." A Southern sophomore believes: "My life will be several levels above my father's. I have a better chance to be successful than he did at my age. I'll be making a better living." Another sophomore said: "If I become a doctor, my financial standing will be higher than my father's. He is a laborer and yet had to send us to school." A Northern college senior noted that "one can make more money today than then." And one of his classmates thinks: "My father probably had to work much harder than I did for equivalent compensation and it will be easier for me as I go along than it was for him."

Then, some made comparisons between their fathers' social milieu and their own. A Northern college senior said: "My father never had any interracial contacts. That's a big difference between us because I have found such contacts to be very broadening." One of his classmates remarked: "My father was chased in Harlem by whites whereas I played with white children." Another member of the same group reported: "My father felt snubbed by the white students at the same high school I attended. The situation there was not as tense for me." A Northern high-school student said that when his father was his age: "I doubt if he had any Jewish and other white friends and I have quite a lot."

Some also commented on the important changes that give them a social advantage over their fathers. A Southern sophomore said: "There are places that I can go that he couldn't go." A Northern high-school senior said: "Things are definitely better for me because today there are laws which protect me which weren't in existence when my father was a young man. Also, the white populace has changed its ideas about Negroes." A Northern high-school senior remarked: "In my father's youth, there was no Civil Rights movement so this situation has to be better for me. It's better for all Negroes now compared to then."

A few youths talked about the effect of military service in World War II upon their fathers' opportunities. "My father had to serve in the Army and go through a war," said one Northern senior. "My prospects are greater." A Northern sophomore related that his father "did attend CCNY, but whatever he had in mind was interrupted by World War II and so he never returned." A classmate whose father's education was also interrupted by the war said: "When he came out of the Army, he did go back but was caught up by the need to work full time and had to give up his college career which he never completed. I expect to finish and end up in a profession." And a Northern high-school senior said: "One major difference is that I do not feel that the prospect of war is as great now as it was when my father was sixteen."

So far the advantages have all been with the younger generation. But a few of our interviewees believe that while the drift is favorable there are some untoward factors which might make their adjustment more difficult, at least in some respects, from that of their fathers.

A Southern sophomore whose father is a mechanic said: "My father had it easier. Mental work is more difficult than manual." A Southern college senior thinks that his chances are about the same as his father's: "He is in education and this field was always open to Negroes." A classmate whose father is also in the educational field recalls: "He often spoke of how it was when he was young. In his profession it was easier than it is now. At that time, there was only the teaching profession. Compared to my father, it will be more difficult to attain my ideals." Still another Southern senior expects things to be harder because "my father is not a professional person." A Northern senior thinks: "It's much harder to get a job now than when my father was a young man because the job market is flooded with dropouts and people who don't go to college."

The full impact of these comparisons made by members of our group between their prospects and those which faced their fathers a generation ago will be seen in the following chapters where we will describe what they hope to accomplish.

4: EDUCATIONAL ASPIRATIONS

Since we selected a group of youths who were either attending college or were college bound, it was hardly surprising to find that they had strong views about the value of educational achievement. If there is one attitude that all of our group share, irrespective of whether they were born and brought up in small or large communities, in the South or in the North, it is the conviction that their future prospects largely depend on the extent of their education. They show considerable awareness that education is becoming the most important route to advancement within American society.

Although many of them told us that their parents strongly encouraged them to aim for high educational goals, several grew up in families where high educational goals were simply assumed to be in the natural order of things. There are a few high-school students who are doing so poorly in their studies that they are concerned about their chances of being accepted by colleges; and there are another few who are not certain about their ability to finance four years of college education. But even these academically weak or financially insecure students hope to go to college and, for that reason, they merit inclusion in this group of college oriented youths.

The concentration on education reflects not only the influence of their parents, but of everybody and everything in their environment. Those with one or both parents with a college degree have direct evidence that their families have been able to reach higher social and economic levels because of the occupational opportunities which education had opened up for their parents, and those with parents with less education have been convinced by their fathers and mothers that a college degree would have opened the way to higher achievements.

Encouragement from their parents has often been reinforced by the experiences of older siblings. For the most part, older brothers and sisters are college oriented. Many were attending college or had already acquired their first degree when our group reached the stage of decision-making with respect to college. This was a strong reinforcement mechanism.

There was often additional support and encouragement from relatives and friends, many of whom had attended and graduated from college or professional school. A young man growing up in an environment in which his parents, older siblings, relatives, and family friends are themselves college graduates or have deep respect and regard for those who are graduates is likely to make college a primary objective.

There has been further reinforcement from the schools which they attended and from the communities in which they were growing up. This reflects two forces: the intensified awareness among American leaders of the critical importance of higher education after the launching of Sputniks and the stress on better educational preparation for Negroes growing out of the Civil Rights movement. From the President of the United States to the classroom teacher, there came a clarion call for more and better educational opportunities.

It is one thing to have an educational goal; it is another to be able to realize it. Realization depends on a variety of conditions and circumstances: the type of elementary and secondary schools available; the individual's scholastic aptitude and performance; the ability to defray the costs of higher education; personal satisfactions derived from learning; and the reactions to experiences within and beyond the classroom. These several dimensions will now be explored.

While we selected high-school students who live either in New York City or Atlanta, a considerable number of the college group are resident students who were born and brought up in other localities. For instance, almost half of our Southern college students come from communities of less than 50,000 population, and another fifth come from cities of between 50,000 and 250,000. On the other hand, about 3 out of 4 of the Northerners are from large metropolitan centers, primarily New York City itself. Since a large proportion of our Northern sample attend City College, which serves local residents almost exclusively, this was to be expected. There were 2 students attending college in the South who live in Northern cities and 4 of those attending Northern colleges who are from the South. For purposes of regional comparison, these 6 students have been included among the youths with whom they attend school, rather than among those who come from the same section of the country, since in selecting their colleges, they have identified themselves, at least temporarily, with the student bodies of those institutions.

Most of the Southerners had attended public elementary and secondary schools and, for most of them, this meant segregated schools since integration has been slow, even in Atlanta and the other large cities of the South. But there are a few exceptions. For instance, a Morehouse sophomore told us: "I went to Mathers Academy. It was integrated—white teachers and colored and white students went there right in Camden, S.C. I was a day student and my parents sent me to this private school. I enjoyed it very much."

But this is unusual, and the following comment is more representative: "I went through the public schools in Ocala, Florida. Teachers were reluctant to help in the Civil Rights movement while I was in high school, but the best teachers did and lost their jobs. Most of the teachers now are not really qualified and the students are discouraged and aren't really learning. We took a test to determine equipment for college when I was in high school and very few Negro students passed. The year I took it only three in my county passed. That was 1962."

This student further remarked that he now finds the program at Morehouse "too rigid considering my high-school background. I am still trying to catch up."

Another told us how handicapped he felt when he first came to college: "I realized my first year in college how much I hadn't had compared to students who had come from high schools out of the South. I went to a pre-college course at Hampton the summer before coming to Morehouse and took math and English and this really helped."

Not a single Southern student made a favorable comment about the quality of his secondary education. Clearly, it left much to be desired.

The Northerners had considerably better educational opportunities. Almost all of them had attended integrated high schools. Moreover, 5 had attended private preparatory schools including such outstanding ones as Kent and Andover. Others had availed themselves of the special high schools in New York: "I more or less exploited the High School of Music and Art as I knew it was high academically. I played the cello in junior high school and this gave me entry to Music and Art."

However, not all of the Northerners are happy with their experiences in high school. Said one: "In high school I didn't think that the teachers encouraged Negro students to get higher education. They didn't show any interest."

Another reported: "I was not given a good conception of what college would be like. It was more difficult than represented. The high-school curriculum was not equally rigorous. At the level of the high-school senior, the college image should be presented more realistically."

One of our high-school students who had once attended de facto segregated elementary schools told us: "I was brought up in Brooklyn. I think I got a poor education there. I think better schools would have made a better student out of me here at ———."

School experience involves much more than classroom instruction and one of our Southern college group who had lived in the North had shifted deliberately from an integrated to a substantially all-Negro high school: "I found out at the elementary school in Buffalo, which I attended from the second through the seventh grades, that race did make a difference in social things. After finishing there, I wanted to go to East High which was predominantly Negro. I went and enjoyed life there and felt that by doing well I could do something for the school and for the race. There was strong rivalry between the Buffalo high schools—in sports, in social affairs, and generally. At first, I had felt ashamed of being a Negro but later on I knew that I was just as good as anyone else. I worked through many changes as president and vice president of the student body and president of the junior class."

Another student at a Southern college had this to report: "I went to public elementary and high schools in Evansville, Indiana. The elementary school was mostly white when I entered but by the time I graduated there were more than 700 Negroes. I went to an all Negro junior high school and spent my senior year at a white high school when the Evansville desegregation plan was at work."

The way in which Sputnik and Civil Rights combined to broaden the opportunities available to certain Negro high-school students is revealed in the following experiences of a young man who is a Morehouse senior: "The summer after my junior year in high school I attended a summer institute sponsored by the National Science Foundation at Morris Brown College. This confirmed my intention to prepare for some work in science. I got early admission to Morehouse at the end of my junior year."

Several other students, primarily in the South, made reference to the fact that they entered college under the early admission plan, an opportunity provided a minority of students who are able to demonstrate that they have successfully mastered preparatory work and who demonstrate a reasonably high order of academic achievement. A sixteen-year-old sophomore reported on his experiences: "I was admitted to Morehouse from the eleventh grade at high school and was offered scholarships by both Morehouse and Fisk. Morehouse was my first choice. My parents wouldn't express an opinion about whether I should accept the early admission scholarship. They let me decide for myself whether to stay and finish high school or come to college. The final decision was difficult because I felt that my age might make some social adjustments difficult."

Another young man who is still in an Atlanta high-school is speeding up his education, not by early admission into college, but by finishing his secondary education more rapidly: "I am advanced in that I took summer school advanced courses, like English and history, so I will finish a year ahead of myself."

A consideration of the colleges which these high-school students plan to attend and of those in which our college students are enrolled gives an indication of the quality of their pre-college schooling and of their scholastic abilities. A principle of inertia frequently operates with respect to college choice, particularly among those who are able to acquire only limited information about the relative quality of institutions of higher learning. Whether one can achieve a college education at a minimum of cost and dislocation is often far more important than the quality of the education itself. Thus, it is not surprising to find that most of the high-school boys, North and South, are planning to attend local colleges. Many Northern boys expect to attend one of the public two- or four-year New York colleges, and many of the Southern boys expect to attend one of three private Atlanta Negro institutions. Although there are several private colleges in the New York area, few boys consider them, primarily because of cost. And although there are integrated Atlanta institutions, few boys consider them, either because of academic ineligibility or of anxieties about personal adjustment.

Several Southern boys expect to go to the colleges the members of their families attended. One boy said: "I have been accepted at Morris Brown College. Daddy and my brother and my cousin all went to Morris Brown and I decided I'd join the group." The Southern Negro alma maters of Northern fathers were rejected by sons who had easy access to superior integrated facilities.

Family sentiment alone does not necessarily provide a complete explanation for choosing their fathers' colleges. These were often local institutions, which would be less expensive than one away from home, and which were likely to look with special favor upon applications from the sons of alumni.

Able Negro students, South and North, are taking advantage of broadened educational opportunities. For example, a seventeen-year-old Atlanta high-school student reported: "Next year I will be a freshman at Yale University. This plan is a cooperative program for educational opportunity which includes eight male colleges and seven female colleges—the Ivy League you know. Two white recruiters came to Atlanta. They have been all over the country to get Negro students to apply to these schools. In the South, they want Negroes. In other sections, they want Mexicans and so on. They gave us forms to fill out to apply for certain schools. I applied to Harvard and Columbia. I also applied to Yale on the side and was accepted there and at Columbia, but not at

Harvard. I want a B.S. degree, a Bachelor of Architecture, that is. I applied to Georgia Tech and was accepted there, but I do not like the environment. I want a Master's at MIT and also a Ph.D. from there. I think I like Yale for undergraduate work. I would go to Morehouse but at Georgia Tech I would be left out of everything."

The same enlarged field of choice is seen for the young man from New York who told us: "I have been accepted at Amherst on the early decision plan. I plan to major in chemistry or biochemistry and I expect to keep going to school until I get a Ph.D. I had considered Harvard, but Amherst accepted me, so I stopped considering Harvard."

Another Northern high-school student said: "I've narrowed it down to five or six colleges. Dartmouth is my number one choice, Columbia is second, Cornell is third, the University of Rochester is fourth, and CCNY is fifth. I have applications ready for all of them and I'll submit them in about a week."

Indicative of students who had limited options because of indifferent grades, limited finances, or both, were the following Northern high-school seniors: "I want to go to Queens Community College and take a two-year nontransfer course in accounting. I can't go to a four-year college because my average is 69. The Queens course would help me get into a career. I would like to go into bookkeeping. I thought of going away to California and living on a campus but my family couldn't afford that even if my marks had been good."

A second, who is a little stronger academically, eventually plans to acquire a degree although he too will first attend a community college: "I am applying for accounting at the New York City Community College. I like what they have to offer and the fee is not expensive. I decided two months ago. My adviser helped me. I am taking a commercial course and my general average is 75. My best subject is accounting; my worst, history. I intend to go there for two years, get good marks, and then transfer to City College."

Typical of a Southern youth without margins is the following young man: "I have application forms to Tuskegee and to Albany State. I haven't written back. I'd rather go into the service. I will get a G.I. bill and it will help me go to school."

In a rapidly changing environment young people are sorely in need of counseling, particularly when doors previously shut are opened and financial assistance previously denied is available. Even the most sophisticated and informed parents find it difficult to give their children the direction they need in making decisions about which colleges to apply to and which subjects to major in.

Only one Southern student mentioned that he had received help from a faculty member in reaching a decision about college. His track coach recommended that he apply for a scholarship to a small college in North Dakota!

On the other hand, the Northern high-school students in our sample have had a considerable amount of educational counseling. One white adviser, also a track coach, appears to have had good rapport with his students. For instance, a boy who was undecided whether to pursue law or pharmacy was given the following list of schools: Toledo, New Mexico, Drake, Howard, Wyoming, and Kansas. "I've narrowed it down to Toledo for law and Drake for pharmacy." Apparently the counselor had developed a list of colleges where average students may be accepted. He appears to have shown interest in every student in his charge. To one who had low marks, he recommended submitting an application to a community college; to another who had no money, he recommended CCNY as the "only school which would give me a degree in engineering without my having to pay tuition."

We have already suggested that, for many, choice of college has been limited because of poor high-school preparation and that, once in college, some feel handicapped because of the inadequacy of their previous education. We have some indication of their scholastic achievement from the school records of the Southern pupils, and from information supplied by the Northerners themselves. Our Southern data is more comprehensive and probably more accurate than the reports of the Northerners.

The Southern high-school students show a wide range of performance: from 2d to 236th out of a class of 300 seniors in one school; and from 9th to 139th out of 195 seniors in the other school. All but 3 students have grade averages of "C" or above but there was only 1 "A" student, the aforementioned Yale entrant. However, since we have no knowledge of the marking systems used in these schools, grade averages alone cannot be used to judge the relative achievement of these students.

On the other hand, scores on national examinations do provide a basis for judgment. We have verbal and mathematical scholastic aptitude test scores for only 6 of the Southern high-school students. Most of the scores are for below the average of college entrants. Since this low standard of performance is also characteristic of the 34 Southern college students for whom we have data, it is evident that a large number of the Southern students have been seriously disadvantaged educationally in comparison with the general college population, and it explains why so many have been severely limited in making college choices.

Although we do not know any of the national test scores of the Northern high-school students, most of them did report their grade averages. Except for 1 "D" student all had averages of "C" or above and half had achieved a "B" average or higher. This is not very different from the Southern high-school records and is consistent with the finding that only about one-third of this group is applying for entrance into colleges with selective admissions policies. Although it is probable that the college preparatory program in a New York City high school is more rigorous than one in segregated Atlanta schools, a better basis for comparison is the type of college they hope to enter, and here the Northerners definitely have the edge. While 8 of the Northern boys believe they are eligible for admission to highly selective institutions such as Amherst, Dartmouth, CCNY, and Columbia, only 1 Southerner has aimed this high. Only 1 other Southern student is considering an integrated college and it is one of low rank.

Comparisons between the scholastic performances of the Northern and Southern college students mean little because of the differences in the institutions they attend. The Northern schools have far higher entrance requirements and more demanding standards of performance than do the Southern ones. Therefore, they attract better students, from both the North and South. More and more of the stronger Southern high-school graduates are being recruited by Northern colleges or are entering recently integrated Southern institutions. This means that the proportion of the ablest at the Negro colleges is generally declining, except possibly for students who receive attractive financial inducements to attend. Few scholastic aptitude test scores of the Southern college students were within a range acceptable to the Northern colleges in the study—Columbia and CCNY, in particular. Of the 68 scores, none was over 600 and there were only six verbal scores and one math score above 500.

The Northern college students, for whom we do not have SAT scores, may be presumed to be stronger scholastically because they had more difficult entrance requirements to meet. Even NYU, whose requirements are not as high as City College's and far lower than Columbia's, would have found few of the Southern youths within its acceptable range. However, it is possible that some Northern students had been accepted on the basis of academic potential rather than actual pre-college achievement, in response to recent policies which provide increased opportunities for Negro students in Northern colleges. In any event, the grades which these boys reported indicate that they have been able to meet the standards of the schools to which they were admitted.

Although our data are suggestive rather than definitive, it is reasonable to conclude that the Northerners as a group are stronger students than the Southerners and that the Northern college students represent the strongest subgroup.

For high-school or college students, the classroom accounts for only one facet of their developmental experience. We have some information about their extracurricular activities and interests. A high-school student said: "There is something about art which permits me to lash out at society, tell life what I think. To me, art is an escape from reality. People dodge and seem so worried about reality. They don't dream any more."

More typical is his classmate who said of himself: "I

am just an average student. I guess I am the athletic type. I play football, basketball, and baseball. I have played from the eighth through the twelfth grades. No, I don't want to be a captain. I am a team man. I get along very nicely with the men on the team."

Another pointed out his difference from the crowd: "I could consider myself a nonconformist. I do not go to rock and roll affairs with other teenagers. I would rather sit home and listen to Bach. I do like pop music, but not the rock and roll type."

Another reported: "I am president of the G.O., a member of the student relations council, the human relations workshop, the orientation program for incoming students, and of the student activities committee."

Among the most active of all the high-school students is a Northerner who reported as follows: "In my spare time, I shoot, bowl, and read. I also play basketball. I play for my church. I am on the basketball squad, the handball squad, and a bowling squad here at school. I also belong to two bowling clubs. Right now I am president of the Methodist Church youth group and I am also a member of the National Rifle Association."

One of his classmates has succeeded in tying together his studies and his avocational interests in such a way that he not only has fun but makes money: "We have a nine-piece dance band and I play the saxophone and clarinet and my brother plays the trumpet and guitar. We make money from dances, etc. I want to major in music."

A picture of a busy Southern college senior was presented by the following young man: "I belong to the glee club, the A.M.S. chorus, the choir, the YMCA, the Student Government Council, the Election Committee, and the Catholic Newman Club."

And another active senior at a neighboring institution reported: "I am on the tennis team at Clark. I am a member of the YMCA and a member of the Omega Pi Phi fraternity. I belong to a math club called the Pythagorean Society. I am a C club man, a letter man, that is. I belong to the athletic club council here at school."

An occasional college student is involved in activities devoted to helping Negroes: "I am planning to join a CCNY group of students and instructors who plan to work with Negro children this summer for the purpose of stimulating them to think about eventually having a college career at CCNY. We intend to approach children at the pre-school and elementary levels via appropriate lectures and also to assist children who have scholastic problems by tutoring."

There are many other facts which tell us how these young people see themselves and the world outside. Some like to read; others are frank to say they do not enjoy reading. Some have become deeply involved in school politics; other believe that heavy involvement may have an adverse effect on their studies. Music, sports, campus politics—these are among the important extra-curricular activities to which they are drawn and from which they derive much satisfaction.

While the United States has long prided itself on the

fact that many youngsters from poor homes have been able to surmount financial barriers to secure a higher education, the fact remains that the amount and quality of education that a young person receives has always been greatly influenced by the ability to pay for it. In general, a student may have his expenses paid by his family; he can be awarded a scholarship; he can work his way through school; or he can borrow funds. Many of these students are financing their education in a combination of ways.

An interesting finding about our group is that in a high proportion of cases the young men's families were the principal sources of support. This is how a Southern high-school senior discussed the question: "I will have no trouble. My father has put money aside and he also has insurance policies that will pay my college fees. My father plans to pay my expenses through college."

Much the same story was presented by a classmate: "My father, who is a postal clerk, will support me through school. He will furnish money for my medical education, too. I need no aid. He said I didn't have anything to worry about, he was going to finance me."

A small refinement of the foregoing is revealed by still another Southern high-school senior: "I'd like to see my father pay my way through school and I'd work for the little things. But anyhow, I would not like to put myself through my educational career."

A Northern lad indicated that he was worried about the stress that his going to college might place on his

widowed mother's resources: "I really don't have a
preference but I would like to stay in the city although
my mother wants me to go away. But I like the city because of the possibilities of working here and therefore
being less of a burden to my mother."

The situation is somewhat different in New York and
Atlanta. Although in both places these students can continue to live at home and thereby considerably cut the
costs of attending college, they must pay tuition in the
South while in New York City they have access to
tuition-free colleges if their marks are high enough.

But the availability of large numbers of scholarships,
both North and South, has further eased the situation.
Here is the report of a Southern senior: "Most of my
financial support has been from scholarship grants and
last year I taught two German classes. I have supported
myself and paid my own schooling all the way through
Morehouse."

Another Morehouse senior reported: "Last year I received a Merrill Fellowship and was sent to study German at a special institute at Colby College during the
summer. I had had a course in German at Morehouse
and was struck with the contrast in teaching methods.
Learning the language at Colby was a pleasure. I then
went to the University of Vienna where I concentrated
on German and philosophy."

The Southern high-school student who has been admitted to Yale plans his financing as follows: "I was
awarded a scholarship at Yale: $550 gift scholarship and

$400 on the job, but I won't work; I don't believe in working my freshman year. A $400 loan, also. That comes to $1,350 financial aid. Then I will get aid from the Board of Regents. They pay for a subject that is not offered in a Negro college. It's still a type of segregation, you know, this new law."

The extent to which the question of money has ceased to be an insuperable barrier for many in our group is suggested by the following Northerner: "I will try for scholarships from the Ford Foundation, State Incentive, the National Negro Fund, and from each school I apply to. My father is willing to help but he can't pay for it all. I'm not too concerned about it because if I don't get a scholarship, I'll get a loan and go to CCNY."

Then the dentist's son who has been admitted to Amherst reported: "I am not eligible for a scholarship because my father earns too much."

About 4 out of every 5 high-school students, North and South, anticipate that all or most of their college expenses will be covered by their families.

For those currently in college, we find that family financing has in fact been a principal source of support, with scholarships for athletic or academic achievements in second place.

Here is the picture at New York University: 2 were admitted on academic scholarships given by the university; 3 are on athletic scholarships, which are granted on an annual basis but are renewable; 1 is on a half-scholarship from the Regents Incentive Program and receives some money from the Samuel Rubin Fund; 1 is on a Ford Scholarship; and 1 is supported by Project Apex, which aids students with potential—he has a five-year scholarship leading to a teaching certificate.

The following are excerpts from the interviews of two students, one from the North and the other from the South, who hold athletic scholarships at New York University: "I entered NYU in the fall of 1963 on an athletic scholarship (basketball) offered on a one year renewable basis for tuition and room. I probably would not have gone to college if I had not received a scholarship. My coach in high school encouraged me to apply for it and so did my mother."

The other reported: "I came to NYU on a basketball scholarship. I came only because I received the scholarship. Ordinarily, I would not have been able to finance an education at a place like NYU. I probably would have ended up in Florida A & M or Tuskegee, for example."

Many of our group attending Columbia or in college in the South are also on scholarships. In the South, the families of a significant minority of our group are paying for all their education; most of the remainder receive some scholarship aid. Very few have taken out loans or are working.

We have seen that most of these young people are growing up in a family and community environment in which going to college has come to be regarded as a necessary and desirable step in the rapidly changing American society and economy. We find, however, that many are attending institutions for reasons of convenience or sentiment and without particular regard to the quality of the education which these colleges provide. Their uncritical view of college seems to have been reinforced by inadequate educational counseling in high school.

Moreover, elementary and secondary schooling is still overwhelmingly segregated in the South, and this fact is important in explaining their poor scores on standardized national tests. The attraction of Negro colleges for these Southern students is more than a matter of family tradition. Only the best of them qualify for admission to the stronger integrated colleges. When qualified Negro students do seek admission to integrated colleges, they are likely to receive partial or full scholarships.

The Northern group has also been handicapped by the quality of their secondary education but not nearly as much as the Southern group. Those with less academic aptitude are able to select from a considerable number of integrated institutions in and out of New York City. The strong students have had access either to prestigious colleges where they were likely to receive scholarships or to the academically strong city college complex which is tuition free. The Northern Negro youngster is able to secure a better education than his Southern counterpart if he has some family support and some aptitude for academic studies.

Notable as is the importance this group attaches to attending and graduating from college, even more striking are their anticipations about post-collegiate education. About 4 out of 5 intend to go beyond the Bachelor's level. The further advanced they are in their education, the higher their aspirations: the high-school students are much more likely to set a Bachelor's degree as their goal than are college students. In fact all but 2 percent of our college seniors plan to go on to graduate or professional school.

Most of those seniors who plan to extend their education to the post-graduate level anticipate attending integrated institutions. This is true not only of almost all of the Northern students, as one could have anticipated, but also of about two-thirds of the Southern college group. However, this is not too surprising since the number of Negro institutions providing strong graduate programs are very few indeed and many fields of specialization are not available at all. Furthermore, the immaturity which may have conditioned many of these youngsters' preference for Negro colleges as protective social environments has been replaced by an eagerness for the challenge and superior learning possibilities of integrated universities.

Students who are about ready to graduate from college expect to finance their further education as they have up to now; through family assistance, scholarships and fellowships, loans, and savings.

A fuller appreciation of this desire for graduate education must await the analysis of their career plans since graduate work is linked to career choice. Up to now, however, we have seen that these middle-class Negroes are fully aware that their best chance of securing their future is through a college education which will give them a springboard for realizing their career plans. Without higher education, a man may achieve high goals but the odds are strongly against him. With a college degree, and particularly with a graduate degree, the odds are on his side.

5: CAREER CHOICES

Most young people are concerned with acquiring a good education because of the leverage that it will provide them in the competitive job world. Career concerns are closely linked to educational planning. This is particularly true of men, since they are expected to be active members of the labor force from the time they complete their schooling.

There are several specific linkages between educational and career planning. In school young people have an opportunity to test their interests and capacities. They acquire certain specific competences which may lead them into particular occupations. They are able to develop and to refine the values and goals which will determine their eventual occupational choices. Finally, they are exposed to teachers and other adults who may influence their career preferences.

However, the occupational choice delineation of young people is not solely a function of their experiences within the educational environment. Other forces are important. There is, for instance, the question of models. Although teachers often are models, youngsters frequently find others outside of the classroom. The family and the neighborhood sometimes provide key career models, since young people are likely to be drawn toward particular careers if they are able to identify with people in those fields.

At the present time young Negroes generally do not have a wealth of useful models. A considerable number of older Negroes are ministers or teachers, but few have achieved high distinction in those areas. Among the more successful Negroes are a limited number of physicians, lawyers, and government administrators. Negroes are poorly represented among businessmen, engineers, scientists, and many other occupations which have long offered substantial economic and social rewards to men in the white community.

Nevertheless, the important fact is not that so few have succeeded, but that some Negroes have been able to succeed despite overwhelming obstacles. Some may have been circumscribed by restrictions which bind them to the Negro community, but within those boundaries they are known and respected. Since they were born into the middle class, our subjects are more likely to be acquainted with these persons than are lower-class youth. They responded affirmatively to these models because the lack of social distance enabled them to identify with them.

On the other hand, young Negroes in college are beginning to realize that they are no longer limited to the few choices that were open to educated Negroes of an earlier generation. Therefore they are attempting to find attractive fields for themselves, frequently without the assistance of established Negro models. One of the concerns of this chapter is to delineate the extent to which the occupational choices of Negro college youth are being modified in response to the reduction and elimination of racial discrimination in employment.

First, we shall review the careers that these students have selected. Next, we shall describe some of their career specifications. We shall then explore the gratifications that they are seeking to realize from their work. By following these several spurs we shall be in a better position to understand the dynamics of their occupational choice.

If we concentrate first on the field of choice of college seniors—as the oldest group their expressed preferences are most likely to be realized—we find that natural science is the selection of approximately a quarter of the students, followed by medicine, with engineering not far behind. This broad array of scientific fields is the first choice of about 3 out of every 5 seniors. The remaining preferences are distributed in descending order as follows: law, social sciences, business, humanities, and education. The most amazing finding, in light of Negro occupational history, is that only one college senior expects to specialize in education per se, although a few consider teaching specific subjects below the college level.

If we compare the tentative choices of the high-school seniors and college sophomores with those of the college seniors, we find differences—but only within broad areas. Thus, we have important evidence that these young people sense the revolution in opportunity that is under way and that they are responding accordingly.

One senior who is about to enter a management training program told us: "At the end of the month, I'll begin working in Detroit at the Chrysler Corporation on a manager training program. For the first two years I'll be on rotation. That is, I will take accounting, data processing, and computer programing. At the end of two years I will be permanently placed in one of these fields, depending upon whether I am successful in dodging the draft."

Another senior limned his prospects as follows: "I plan to work as a technician on an assembly line, some type of skilled factory line. Lockheed here has training courses. The company will send you to school in the summers and give you a job in the winter. I would like to do one specific job, so when I finish my senior year I would then become oriented in the job at Lockheed with preliminary training on the job. Then they would pay me to go to Tech or to Emory and . . . after you finish you can get the real important jobs like working as an engineer in this organization. . . . The field is so wide I can plan to work in a factory or else work in physics in the field of computer mechanics."

A Northern college sophomore is weighing three general alternatives but with a considerable degree of practicality: "I have three choices—actuarial work, which doesn't necessarily require a graduate degree, computer programming, and teaching. The last two do require a second degree. The first, actuarial work, requires extensive experience in order to get ahead, this is, in terms of making a big salary. My first choice is to go into the insurance field as an actuary. This doesn't mean that I'm against a graduate school, but that I prefer actuarial work over computer programming or teaching. If my grades are very good when I graduate in 1967, I will probably go to graduate school and do advanced work in math. If not, I'll go for an actuarial job and consider evening graduate school."

A young Southern high-school senior is aiming very high: "I want to work for the federal government. . . . I am interested in government research and want to be a research lawyer and a staff worker in the National Labor Relations Board. My next choice is in the State Department handling foreign affairs. Then, later, when I am older, I would like to go into politics, national politics, of course. I know you will laugh, but my final ambition is to become a member of the Supreme Court. First, I'll be a representative, a Senator for my state, then a member of the Cabinet, then Attorney General, and then become a member of the Supreme Court."

A key consideration in a study of occupational choice is to get some sense of how realistically a young person has approached the problem in terms of his own interests and abilities and of the opportunities available to him. The following excerpts reveal this.

A Southern high-school senior has strong pulls to medicine but also some strong aversions: "I will become a psychiatrist. First I decided to be a doctor, but I do not like organic functions. My father is a surgeon and I thought about my father's being called out at night, so I decided against that. I decided that I make friends easily so I am compatible. By being a psychiatrist I wouldn't have to operate on people, but I guess tampering with the mind can be as dangerous as cutting."

Recognizing both the need and the opportunity a Southern sophomore is fairly well set on what he wants to become: "I hope to go into social work or counseling of some sort. I believe it's an open field and on the basis of my experience in the Civil Rights movement, particularly in Americus, I know there are so many things which need to be done. So few people seem to be concerned about the basic social problems, especially about the problems of people in rural areas."

A Northern sophomore looks forward to being in a more influential position: "I'm interested in the social sciences mostly because I have an interest in the racial problem and I can see myself effecting change through education, psychology, and sociology. At fifteen I noticed that I enjoyed working with people; and my family has always been interested in education, especially my father, mother, and oldest sister. . . . I intend to take a Master's in psychology with the goal of becoming school psychologist. I want to be in a position to influence an entire school system. I would work in any city with a large Negro population. As a later goal I would like to be a consultant to a school board or boards where my ideas might influence a whole school."

There is another Northern sophomore who has had his eye on a career in the Air Force for a long time and he is moving right along to realize his goal: "I want to go into the AAF as a career. When I was nine or ten, I knew I wanted to go into the Air Force. I wanted to be a pilot. Right now I'm majoring in bio since I figured I'd get my best marks in it. You could even be an accounting major, as are some fellows in the ROTC now who plan to become pilots next year. I'll be twenty-three after I get my M.S. and I expect to get a captain's commission."

Some youngsters must cope with dual forces—what they like as well as what their parents like for them —such as another Northern college sophomore: "When I was nine, I spent five months in the hospital with rheumatoid arthritis. I fully recovered. I had a lot of opportunity to observe doctors. But before I was nine, I wanted to be a history teacher. I was fascinated by the past. I talked quite a lot about this at home, but my parents dissuaded me on the basis of it's not being a lucrative field at that time. They encouraged me to enter medicine and I went along with it. Later I discovered that I didn't like biology—no, it wasn't a question of scholarship. I just didn't take to the subject matter and at that point I rejected medicine. I found myself thinking of history in terms of law—corporate law, international law, or the diplomatic service. I intend to go to law school but I haven't decided on a specialty. Each seems attractive right now."

A Northern high-school senior told how he juggled such alternatives as law, business, and economics, and decided among them: "When I entered high school I knew I wanted to go to college so I began to consider the possibilities. I thought of being a lawyer. I felt that being a lawyer was a good possibility but that economics would be better in terms of opportunities. In high school I found out that there were more jobs in the business world in economics than any other field of liberal arts except education. Subsequently, I heard a guidance counselor state a similar point to a student. I forgot about law and saw economics as a semi-scientific course of study employing formulas and it seemed more challenging than history or English."

Further evidence of the degree of realism with which these young people approach the question of their future work is demonstrated by practical considerations taken into account by older students who have recently made shifts in their plans.

A sophomore recently changed his goal from medicine to dentistry. He reported: "This year I changed from wanting to be a doctor to wanting to be a dentist. For one thing, I don't have to specialize and it will not take quite as long to study dentistry as it would to study medicine."

A classmate decided that biological research is a less

rocky road than medicine: "I want to be a doctor, but I've been thinking that the professional training is too long and too expensive. I may work awhile and then go to graduate school. My major is biology. I may plan to go into biological research. My main reason for questioning medicine is the matter of time and money."

A senior related a more or less typical story of a gradual transition from a fantasy to a realistic career choice: "When I was young, I wanted to be an astronomer. I read books about astronomy. Then I passed through the soldier phase, which I call my military phase. During high school, my aunts encouraged me to enter medicine, but this was totally out of the question. I didn't have the mental ability to step into medicine. It was too alien to my own ideas. I compromised with them so I entered physics, which was my first major. I changed because I didn't think I possessed the dedication to work in a laboratory. There was no contact with people. So now I'm in business administration."

A high-school senior who still has time before him to make additional shifts is already far on the way to a definite choice: "I had first thought of being an engineer back in the eighth grade. I like to build things and I liked math and sciences. I switched to accounting. I didn't do as well in my math as I wanted to, so I switched my major. I like math, and accounting is related. I am not enthused about accounting, but I am interested. I am taking it now; I like it; and I am doing well in it."

Some young men have approached the question of their occupational futures by realistically assessing the alternatives which they face with regard to graduate education. A Columbia sophomore said: "I intend to enter law school on graduation. Yale is my first choice because the curriculum is easier, Columbia is my second, and Harvard is third but hazardous since the attrition is greatest—that is, a class of 500 dwindles to 350. NYU is my fourth choice. As far as financing is concerned, I anticipate fellowships, scholarships, and parental assistance. After law school I plan to take the Bar. After the Bar I plan to go to business school for six months and take intensive courses in banking."

Another Columbia senior is determined to acquire at least a Ph.D. and apparently will have no particular difficulties in doing so: "The most important aspect of my future is to continue my education until I acquire at least a Ph.D. I have been offered a faculty fellowship at $250 a month, a teaching fellowship at Michigan, and the Engineers Joint Council has offered me a practical trainingship for a minimal period of two to six months. I would be working for Shell Petroleum, and I will probably undertake the trainingship and, upon its completion, the faculty fellowship at Columbia."

A third classmate whose home is in the South is attempting to decide whether to attend medical school in the North or South: "My present plan is to go to medical school and study psychiatry. The immediate problem is whether I'll go to medical school in the

North or the South. If North, I would choose NYU,
Downstate, or Western Reserve. If South, Duke, North
Carolina, or Bowman Gray. I'm torn right now."

Since so many of these youngsters are from families
that are not able to guide them vocationally and since
many did not receive much systematic guidance in
school, it is striking that they were able to do so well in
formulating satisfactory career plans for themselves.

It is illuminating to consider, if only briefly, whether
the choices of these young people took into account
their capacities, at least as they were reflected by the
marks that they achieved in school. It is also relevant to
consider more carefully the functions they hope to perform in their fields and the institutional framework
within which they expect to work.

Since there were only 6 "A" and 8 "D" students in the
entire group, the important distinction is between the
"B" and the "C" students. We find that 3 out of 4 of
those majoring in the natural sciences are at least "B"
students, as are 3 out of 5 who looked forward to studying medicine. The less able students are concentrated in
the social sciences, business, and engineering. While it
might be invidious to say that weaker students are more
likely to make their way in the latter fields, it is safe to
contend that only "B" students have much chance for
success in science and medicine. To the extent that
marks afford a clue, these young men are thinking quite
sensibly about the fields in which they are likely to
succeed.

Let us consider the type of work that they see themselves doing in the future and the environment within which they expect to work. Somewhat more than a quarter of the entire group anticipate following professional careers in which they will be self-employed. About the same proportion look forward to holding down staff positions in business. A slightly smaller group hope to have careers in university teaching and research or in teaching at a lower level in the educational structure. The remainder expect to be owners or managers of business enterprises, or administrators or staff members in nonprofit institutions or in the government. The striking facts that emerge from these specifications are that several youths anticipate that they will have positions in corporate management; that a significant minority look forward to reaching responsible staff posts in business; and finally, that a large number aspire to university careers.

These are all employment settings that have traditionally been closed to Negroes except where the institutions themselves were Negro owned or operated. That they are the goal of so many of these youths is an indication that recent moves toward integration of administrative, managerial, and professional staffs are breaking down barriers to the aspirations of Negroes.

However, a large number of students, primarily prospective doctors and lawyers, would like to be self-employed. This goal has become less popular among white students who see the practice of medicine and law as increasingly institutionalized and who prefer security and freedom from pressure as employed professionals in preference to the responsibility and hazards of self-employment. But for Negroes, the local doctor and lawyer have often been admired community leaders who function with a measure of personal independence that no organizational employment provides, particularly to members of their race. Thus, there appears to be an understandable lag between the downgrading of the self-employed professional among whites and his continuing high esteem among Negroes.

Another dimension of the career choices of these Negro youths is the gratifications that they seek to realize in their future work. About half of the group stress such factors as the nature of the career field itself, the challenge of the work or the interpersonal relations on the job—all of which relate to values that derive mutually from work and from one's own interests and values.

Next in importance are those gratifying aspects mentioned by almost 2 out of 5 students which concern extrinsic factors such as income, prestige, conditions of work, and future opportunities. The remaining students, about 1 in 6, state that they have chosen a field in which they can be of service, either to people generally, or to Negroes specifically.

The important conclusion to be drawn from this distribution is that a large number of young men—roughly 3 out of 5—are choosing careers solely on the basis of personal satisfaction without reference to more objective factors. They believe that they can choose careers in terms of values that are important to them and that they are no longer under the same pressure as their parents or grandparents who had to take whatever opportunities happened to be available without regard to personal preferences.

But this much expanded occupational horizon with its many new opportunities is not an unmixed blessing. Most young people find it difficult to undergo a process of weighing and discarding alternatives until they finally make a more or less permanent choice. Negro youngsters find it more difficult than their white classmates, because so many of the opportunities now available to them were not previously open to their relatives, their friends, or their teachers. Consequently, they can receive little guidance from these sources.

This is what some of them told us about their parents' attitudes toward their plans. In some cases, their parents followed a hands-off policy, as in the case of a Northern college sophomore: "Becoming a pilot is mostly my baby. My parents couldn't care less and I don't really like people telling me what to do. I like to figure out things myself."

Two other Northern college youths also reported that they had made their decisions without any encouragement from home. One said: "I have decided on medicine. I received no encouragement or inspiration from home. I had to work out what I wanted to do in my own mind. I expect to finance medical school by taking a loan from a bank." The other reported: "My parents have played no part in my career plans. I didn't talk to them—I just told them what I wanted to do. I remember that when I was still a child I used to say I wanted to be a writer, but this idea was never encouraged."

The parents of others played a major role in their decisions. For instance, a Southern senior heading for medicine said: "My parents are all for my plans. We have a doctor in the family and they say, 'We'll have a new doctor in the family at last.' My father was in medical school. It was a very trying experience and he did not finish, but my uncle continued so that my parents are all for my becoming a doctor."

Another Southern senior reported: "My father always said, 'You can win the Nobel prize.' All the members of my family as well as the faculty at school encouraged me to go into science."

In some situations the parents push in one direction and the young men are influenced but not persuaded. A Southern high-school senior simply avoids discussion, or at least conflict: "I want to be a psychiatrist. My parents and I have had no discussions in depth, but I don't want to argue with them. They think I will change my mind and become a surgeon so I just skip it."

Evasion is not quite so easy for the Morehouse sophomore who said: "It is hard for me. I really need someone to talk to who understands my problems. My parents don't quite understand. I hate to do anything that they do not wish me to do. I think they would like for me to be a doctor and not a French professor as I would prefer."

One young man interpreted the source of conflict between himself and his parents: "My family puts pressure on me to complete my work at Morehouse, which means continuing in chemistry from which I now want to change. I believe the majority of Negro families who have had little money put emphasis on getting in and getting out and earning. There is very little support for a change of major."

Clearly many parents play a role in the choices which their sons make. Some seek to stop their children from aspiring too high or from pursuing fields in which they will encounter difficulties. Others, pleased with their sons' prospective choices, are supportive, and others simply consider it best not to interfere.

Although parents are often influential persons in a young man's occupational decision-making, others occasionally play a determining role. A Northern sophomore identified the key persons who influenced his choice: "The critical people responsible for shaping my outlook are my godfather, who is a professor of anthropology at Columbia and who raised my horizons about history and law; my stepfather and mother, who have always been interested in my achieving a career; and an official at the Urban League. I knew her daughter, and in going to her house, I met a lot of interesting people and mixed quite a lot with varying social and cultural groups."

Sometimes a teacher was central: "In the eighth grade I had a history teacher who was an English lady. She liked me and encouraged me to think about becoming a history teacher. I decided then that I would become one."

Another reported: "In high school, one of the greatest teachers I have ever had, a chemistry teacher, inspired me tremendously, and I decided then that I wanted to be a chemist."

Still another had this to say: "There was a Negro French teacher in high school and she inspired me to become a teacher. Since I was specializing in biology and was doing well, I made a decision that I would prepare to become a high-school biology teacher."

Friends and acquaintances often play an important role: "When I went to Boston with the glee club I stayed with a doctor who was just out of medical school and he gave me pointers. He was a recent graduate and made me more sure about becoming a doctor. You see, my uncle finished in 1940 and this young man in 1959. There was almost nineteen years difference and several changes had been made in this field which really helped me to decide."

Another heading for medicine said: "There are many examples. There were doctors in the community. It was the way they carried themselves. A doctor in a small community is strangely set apart. People trust one man and go to him for help in solving their problems, problems that have nothing to do with medicine. They have an outstanding and strong influence in the community. And so this kind of man inspires respect in so many small communities."

Occasionally, a young man referred to the influence of nationally known figures as evidence that certain fields had become open to Negroes and that Negroes could achieve eminence in established fields. "There is a Bob Teague on NBC news who is a news reporter. I first saw him this summer at the California convention over TV. That was the first time I had seen a Negro on TV newscasting. It did show me some openings that would be available in that field."

Another said: "As a young boy I developed an interest in the judiciary field, in law. People like Thurgood Marshall, Powell, and Edward Brooke, the attorney general in Massachusetts, have influenced me."

In addition to parents and other key persons, young people are frequently helped to clarify their occupational choices through formal or informal guidance and counseling. The young men in our group referred both to the guidance they received and the guidance they wanted but which was not forthcoming.

A Southern high-school senior reported about the guidance to which he had been exposed: "I want to be a C.P.A. That was my first choice. I have also thought of working in insurance, in the actuary department. A teacher of mine gave us booklets about being a C.P.A., but I have had no counseling about what is involved in being an actuary."

A Northern high-school senior learned about the educational prerequisites for aeronautical engineering from his school counselor: "When I first settled on aeronautical engineering, I spoke to the counselor here and he told me that I would not only have to continue my education by going to college, but that I would probably have to take graduate courses also. I plan to do that."

A Northern high-school senior reported: "When I was younger, before high school, I thought about being a lawyer or a writer, but my father said it was hard to get into the law field. My average in English is 75 to 80 and my English teacher said it would be better if I went into something else. I talked about it with my adviser and he agreed I should go into music since that was my love. That is when I decided to go into music."

Another young Northerner had helpful teachers: "In junior high school I found that I liked ceramics in the industrial arts class. I want to go into ceramics engineering. The teachers here have encouraged me to go for a scholarship and I got one at Alfred."

On occasion, a school official can push so hard that the young person balks at his advice: "When I was a child a strange thing happened. I wanted to be a doctor but my principal in high school pushed me too hard. He obtained a six-year scholarship for me at Boston University. This was a six-year combined college and medical school. As good as their offer was I disliked being pushed and so I turned it down."

A Northern college senior told us: "When I came to

New York ten years ago, I didn't have the slightest idea of what to do in terms of a career. But in junior high school, high school, and college, I received sufficient information to help me to make up my mind."

Another Northerner, a college sophomore, also reported that his counselor had been helpful: "I would say that I got good guidance—I was even informed about scholarship opportunities available to Negroes."

Another offered a mixed report: "At C——— High School I was offered a scholarship to a Catholic university but no help in working out a career."

Against this generally positive assessment of the help received from teachers and counselors in clarifying their educational and career plans must be placed the considerable negative testimony offered by many.

A Northern student now in college reported his experience and his reactions to them: "I think that representative college courses should be given in the senior year in high school so that students will know more about the challenge of college courses. I also think there should be more guidance in high school. I feel that part of my problem was not knowing what to expect."

A CCNY senior talked about his earlier experiences in the New York City school system: "There should be more guidance at the high-school level. I was not advised to go to college. The guidance man just wanted to get me out of the school. The emphasis was that I now had a high-school diploma and I could get a good job. While this didn't affect me, it could frustrate other Negro children. The prevalence of social problems, such as delinquency, interferes with the advisory function. No one ever mentioned scholarships to me. It was just assumed that I would not go to college."

A few young men explicitly stated that they believed that more could be done with the use of psychometric instruments to help students clarify their career objectives: "I wish college could have offered an aptitude test to give us at least a general idea of our capabilities. I believe that the counseling system at Morehouse is very inadequate. There is no opportunity to find out about requirements or possibilities in various fields. The Placement Office provides booklets but little else. I have had no occupational guidance."

In some cases, the scores that a young man received on his aptitude test caused him to alter his choice: "I originally wanted to go into engineering when I was fourteen. I liked math and science and thought this would be best applied in engineering. Several friends of the family were engineers and they influenced my choice. . . . In the ninth grade in high school I took aptitude tests. All grades were high except mechanical ability. I was told that the 56th percentile was not good enough for engineering. So I changed to chemistry in which I had a 95 average in high school."

A Southern college senior thinks that being Negro negatively affected the quality of his guidance: "If I were white, I'd probably have had more help in making plans. My high-school counselor concentrated on keeping students in school and urging them to go to college. Individual teachers stressed opportunities in teaching. I came to college looking for something else because I regard teaching as a last resort. My high school provided nothing except career days when job choices in general were discussed. I think the personnel department at college should offer students work opportunities related to career plans, more for experience than for money."

The young men in our study gave us a wide range of reactions to the extent and quality of guidance they received. A minority encountered no special difficulties in clarifying their occupational choice and in taking the right steps to pursue it. Another group received considerable positive support and encouragement from home, and they too were able to find their direction without too much trouble.

Still others were lucky enough to have friends or acquaintances who helped them to clarify their ideas about the future. But there were a great many—probably a majority of the entire group—who needed help from teachers and counselors. Some got help and, for the most part, it was constructive. But more reported an absence of information, testing, and counseling. They were left to resolve their own uncertainties without a helping hand either from their classroom instructors or from staff counselors.

While better or more guidance may be a matter of some significance in the developmental experiences of all young people, the role of race in the decision-making process of most young Negroes can be determining. Minorities, faced with discrimination, often must forgo utilizing their potential and education and settle for second or third best since the preferred positions in society are arbitrarily closed to them. This points to the importance of considering the principal obstacles in the process of occupational choice determination of these Negro youth.

Most of these young men referred to some obstacle that might interfere with the realization of their occupational goals, but few anticipated being blocked completely. They called attention to a miscellany of factors: limitations of money to finance an extended period of graduate or professional study, uncertainty as to whether they possess the intellectual capabilities or specific aptitudes required to perform at a high level of competence in a chosen field, and problems of personality which might make it difficult for them to persevere under the frustrations of a long and arduous course of studies. These were the principal types of obstacles which the young men think might upset their plans. While the college seniors appear to be a little more aware of possible obstacles in their path—they were closer to the world of work—the overriding impression, despite notes of caution, is one of quiet confidence.

This is revealed in the following statements by three Southern college men: A sophomore who hopes to be a dentist said: "I am pretty sure of my ability." A senior whose goal is to be a systems engineer remarked: "I will have a fairly easy time because I think I have the mental capacity to do this job." A sophomore who plans to be a doctor said: "It will be fairly easy. The work is difficult in this field, but no more difficult than anywhere else."

Dedication to their occupational goal was considered by two other Southern college men to be a sound basis for optimism. A senior who wishes to be a doctor said: "It will not be too difficult. If you like what you are doing, it is not hard but worthwhile." A sophomore noted: "I've been interested in music all my life. I can't think of anything that would prevent my going on in music."

Some have considered the employment market and perceive it in favorable terms. A Northern high-school senior said: "I chose business administration because it is such a wide field." A Southern college sophomore who plans to become an electrical engineer remarked: "Many industries are opening up for Negroes so it will be fairly easy to get into this field." A Southern high-school senior said: "I will make it, I believe. In time, by hard work I will make money. I will do things better because I am a Negro and have white competition. This competition will not stop me but will only make me work harder for the future."

Some students believe that their future depends very much on their own efforts. A Northern sophomore who plans to be a C.P.A. believes that "there are no obstacles other than myself."

A Northern high-school senior who is undecided about

whether to follow law or pharmacy sees no obstacle "except making up my mind." A Southern high-school senior said: "I am ambitious and I feel I can be something if I want to be." A Southern senior who expects to enter finance remarked: "I'll have an easy time. All that is necessary will be a good performance and favorable impressions. I'm a little conceited about myself."

One might almost see cockiness in the prospective psychologist who said that "nothing is keeping me back," and in the budding chemist who said: "I feel that my opportunities are unlimited right now. I feel I have the ability to do the work and don't foresee any discrimination which will affect me. I feel confident that I have the mental ability."

So much for the optimists. Some of the group, of course, see problems ahead. Several referred to financial problems. A Southern sophomore whose aim is to be a research chemist believes: "Financially it will be hard. I am an honor roll student but I need financial backing badly." A Northern college senior said: "The financial aspect is the real obstacle. When I come out of the service, I will have to go to work in the best-paying job that is available and arrange to go to law school at night." A Southern college senior whose goal is medicine reported: "It is difficult in the sense that I do need necessary funds. Otherwise, there is no problem as far as intellectual background is concerned."

Some had doubts about themselves, particularly about their desire and ability to stay with their studies. A

Northern senior who is planning to become a physician said: "I do feel apprehensive about the grind in terms of my ability to see it through." One of his classmates who wishes to be a history teacher reported: "I don't foresee any obstacles except my own feelings of indecision which I have to contend with sometimes." A Southern college senior who hopes to be a lawyer feels: "I will be able to carry out my plans but it will not be easy. Any field you enter is hard at first. You must apply yourself." A classmate whose goal is aeronautical engineering realizes: "It requires hard work since the field is so new and broad. I am sure of myself and my ability, but to work at a job of this kind takes real dedication and I'm not quite sure I am dedicated to this extent."

From what these students, the confident ones and the doubtful, have revealed about themselves, we can see that they are little different from any other group of adolescents and young adults from middle-class backgrounds. They are neither unduly self-confident nor overly anxious about themselves and their future.

We have left to the last their feelings about the element of race and whether they attribute much importance to it in shaping their choices or in their ability to implement them. The quotations presented above, most of them silent about race, suggest that many of our youngsters did not consider it very important in their decision-making. Even when an occasional student mentioned the racial obstacle he was likely to conclude that, on balance, he would be able to surmount it without undue trouble.

A Southern senior who anticipates a career in real estate believes: "The future will become more and more competitive as racial conditions change. There will be more opportunities but higher requirements. However, a Negro with ability and drive will have a pretty good chance." A Northern college senior who plans to practice law in Atlanta said that the only obstacle he can see is "the hazard of a Negro living in the South and competing with white lawyers who command greater acceptance." A Southern college senior, an aspiring doctor, thinks he will have to contend with "the preconceived notions about Negroes. The patients at the hospitals will probably draw back and think only that I am a Negro. But, student-like, I hope to be able to conquer their dislike."

There are two ways of interpreting this underplaying of the racial factor in their expectations. One is to see it as evidence of their immaturity and naïveté in face of the continued difficulties experienced by Negroes in overcoming restrictive policies. The other is to see these Negro college men as eminently realistic in so far as their awareness of new opportunities for educated Negroes is concerned. They do not say that they expect never to encounter discrimination, either in preparing for their careers or in pursuing them. But they do suggest that they expect to achieve their plans. That they are Negroes is no longer the crucial factor. Whether these young people are naïve or realistic will be known only in the future. But it is likely that their relaxation about the racial element is sound, if only because of the growing demand for the skills of the well trained. Furthermore, it runs counter to Negro experience to err on the side of optimism.

Now that we have the wide range of considerations influencing these young men in their approach to career choice, we shall briefly summarize the key facts that have become clear. By and large the parents of these young Negroes, like the parents of middle-class white college students, play a part—but not the determining part—in the way their offspring approach their occupational choices. While a few may insist that their sons prepare for specific occupations, most of them are willing to assume positions on the side lines. They proffer advice when asked, they offer their criticisms in muted tones, and in general they are supportive.

The second important fact is that the conventional middle-class Negro vocational choices of elementary and secondary school teaching and the ministry have receded far into the background, and in their place one finds such new fields as business management, science, and engineering. These young people have made their choices with considerable awareness of the new opportunities. In fact, only a very few give consideration to matters of race in weighing alternatives.

These young men will find it difficult to exploit fully

the new opportunities since there are few models in their immediate families or environs who can help them learn about styles of work and the best ways of getting prepared. In addition, the counseling that they have received in school is frequently inadequate. Nevertheless, in one way or another, they are achieving that knowledge about the unknown which they need to get themselves pointed in the right direction.

For the most part their career goals are realistic. One young man may aspire to become a justice of the Supreme Court, and another hopes that he may some day be president of General Motors. But these are dreams, not serious plans. Most of the group are much more modest. They seek to enter fields within their competence and grasp.

The extent of their broadened opportunities is best revealed by the fact that when they consider their life work, they weigh not only such mundane matters as prospective income and opportunities for promotion but whether their careers will enable them to gain direct satisfaction from their work, irrespective of monetary rewards. Like many other educated people they want meaningful and challenging work and they expect to find it.

6: LIFE GOALS

Although the choice of a life's work is a central concern of young males, they see it as one of several dimensions of the future. Fundamental to their career choices and to all their other goals are the kinds of lives they wish to lead.

We have described some of the decisions which our young men have made about their future lives. They anticipate extensive schooling and have chosen careers at the top of the occupational ladder. Certainly they know their place in the economy is basic to the accomplishment of their other goals.

What are these other goals? Some are directly related to their occupational choice—they specify the manner and the circumstances in which they hope to pursue their careers and the levels of competence and advancement which they hope to achieve. Others concern their personal lives. They center upon marriage and family and the broader social environment. Some involve both personal and career factors—such as standard of living and place of residence. Like their career choices, all of these goals are based on individual values modified by interests, aptitudes and personal influences. The composite of these goals represents a youth's picture of himself in the future.

The majority of these young men, especially those in college, have had an increasingly clear perception of the types of lives that they look forward to leading; as they have matured, their values have become clearer and have helped to give them direction. In this chapter we will review their conception of their own futures and also their aims and aspirations for their wives and for their children.

We have discussed these youths' occupational choices. We shall now consider how they expect to translate these choices into viable careers. The following quotations are limited to the college group, since they are much further along in the crystallization of their career plans.

A Northern sophomore outlined the progression that he hopes to follow: "I am attracted to international banking. I would like to work for either a large corporation or a large banking institution as a lawyer. In the field of international banking I would expect a starting salary of $10,000 and in ten years, $20,000 and, by retirement, $50,000."

Another sophomore has clear aims: "My goal is to be a C.P.A. It's my intention to take the C.P.A. qualifying exam. I would like to work for the Internal Revenue Service in a northeastern location. While working I intend to go after an M.B.A. After that I'll probably earn more money, just how much I don't know."

A Southern college sophomore has bright hopes: "I want to achieve a respectable position in society, to teach and to be a first-rate performer, respected and admired as a person. I would like to become not a good Negro pianist, but a good pianist. Whatever I become is really up to me."

Another Southern college student said: "I don't want to go into private law practice. I want to get a steady job with a fixed amount of income. I believe that Negroes now will be generally better prepared and although it's hard to get into high positions in corporations, I believe if I work hard I can make it."

A Southern college senior who plans to enter medicine has quite a detailed plan worked out: "My plans are to go back to Africa for one year of internship and then teach and do research at one of their colleges. From there I will probably come back home and teach and do research at the University of Florida. I won't make but $15,000 a year. Really, the money part isn't too important because my joy will be working in a research laboratory."

A senior has the following goals in the field of law: "I want to major in criminal law and practice in New York State. After law school I will take the Bar and get hitched up with some law firm that's bigger than a one-man office. The ultimate assignment I want is to specialize in courtroom law; that is, presenting and defending cases in an affiliation with the law firm unless it became evident from the turn of events that I could open my own office."

Another Northern senior looks forward to employment in a large corporation: "As a chemical engineer, I would like to design refinery equipment and work out refinery processes. The latter is probably related to photography and film development in which I was very interested when I was thirteen and fourteen. I would like to work for a petroleum company like Standard or Esso. I would not object to an assignment which involved travel as I have no plans to get married, although at first I would try to get work in a geographical area where I could continue my education."

A considerable number of the group specified their future employers. We have already quoted some who look forward to working for government, for a large law office, or for a corporation.

A Northern sophomore had learned abut the prospects for employment in his field: "I am primarily interested in abnormal psychology and I found out that positions are available for this kind of work in corrective institutions for mentally disturbed children. I intend to take state exams for jobs in institutional settings."

Another Northerner, a senior, hopes to work for a nonprofit organization: "I'm not sure that I want to practice law in the conventional sense. Ideally, I'd like to connect with some international organization like the U.N., the World Health Organization, or teach inernational law or work for the government."

A third looks forward to holding down two part-time jobs: "I would like to work in New York as a pathologist in a hospital, while working simultaneously on a part-time basis as a general practitioner in private practice."

A capable young scientist is modeling himself after one of his professors: "The particular branch of chemistry in which I plan to specialize involves mathematical and physical applications of chemistry. . . . With a Ph.D. one is involved in more interesting work, and one teaches at a university level. At the same time I would probably be involved in consulting work. From teaching and consulting, professors at Columbia must command an income of about $30,000."

These brief quotations tell us about the career plans of the college group and the type of work situations in which they hope to find themselves. Remarks about their anticipations concerning future income were incidental. But we sought information on this point from the entire group; one reason was to determine how much knowledge they had about the world of work and to what extent their plans for their future lives were based on realistic formulations. Here is what various high-school students anticipated with regard to future incomes:

"At twenty-five, I should be through with college and, if I am successful with math, maybe I would like to work with computers. I can't think of a company offhand. I would be earning between $15,000 and $20,000 a year. That might require a B.S. degree. I said fifteen to twenty because I know there will be inflation by then."

"My specialty would be civil engineering. I would work for a private concern. I would expect $10,000 to

$15,000 to start and in ten years $25,000 to $30,000."

"As a 2d lieutenant I would draw $222 a month. A general gets $1,200. I suppose to aim at being a major or lieutenant colonel would be a more realistic goal."

"I'm planning tentatively to work in private industry, possibly in advertising research. With an M.A., I would expect about $15,000. If I'm successful at it, my income later on would be unlimited."

"I think I would like to be in the pharmacy field at a drug store making about $5,000 as a pharmacist up to $40,000 as an owner-pharmacist."

"If I am good, my income as a musician should be quite high, about $250 a week. If I am not good, I can always teach. There would be other income from recitals here and there, that is if I am good, and there would probably be income from church in terms of playing the organ. I am not really worried about income. I think I would make out O.K."

"I would want to earn anywhere between $110 and $140 a week. I think that's how much it would take to support a family of four people. I think my father's earnings are in this bracket and there are six people in the family and we're doing pretty good financially."

We are impressed with several qualities manifested by the responses of these young people. First, they have a considerable amount of solid information about the current wage and salary structure. Next, they appreciate the wide range which exists in many fields which makes them quite uncertain as to what they will eventually be able to earn. Finally, there is a sense of optimism. They are not worried about being able to earn a good living.

What can be added by the replies of the college group? The following excerpts are from Northerners:

"I would like to get a job in experimental biological research and then go for an M.S. I could probably get a job as a technician or lab assistant at $5,000 to $6,000 a year. I haven't looked into the money angle, but with an M.S. I would expect $7,500 to $8,500. I feel the emphasis should be getting myself placed rather than on the money."

"I would expect to earn about $5,600 to $5,800 as a math teacher, which is my first choice, and about $6,500 to $7,000 as an airline navigator. At age thirty, I would expect to be earning in excess of $7,500. I have never been interested in earning a lot of money, but I am beginning to be more realistic about the importance of money."

"I anticipate practicing law in Harlem and I would imagine my income would fluctuate between $7,500 and $9,000 and that this would not drastically change, even in ten years, as I would still be working in Harlem among individuals with low incomes."

"As far as financial return is concerned, I have heard that income in the medical profession is lucrative. Once established I would expect $15,000 to $20,000, and in about ten years, about double that."

And the Southerners:

"I hope to earn $20,000 a year after about a year or so of dental practice."

"I hope to be a Mississippi senator. I want money. You don't make much money as a state senator, only about $3,000 a year, so I would also have to have a private law practice which would yield about $5,000 or $6,000 a year, and after a while I will be earning around $12,000 a year."

"I would like to make around $60,000 a year. However, you'd have to be pretty well established to make this amount of money, so by 1976 I expect to be making quite a large sum of money as a medical specialist."

This is how the group as a whole sees its financial future. We have data for approximately two-thirds of the entire group. About 15 percent anticipate earning less than $10,000; the largest number, about 1 in 3, anticipate an income of between $10,000 and $15,000. Another substantial group, 1 in 4, expects to earn between $15,000 and $20,000. About 20 percent look forward to incomes of between $20,000 and $50,000, and another 10 percent have still higher expectations.

While at first one might be inclined to think that these youngsters are overestimating themselves, a closer look suggests that this is not necessarily so. There are 7 out of 10 who do not anticipate earning in excess of $20,000, and some have even made allowance in their estimates for an inflationary factor. In addition, among those who anticipate large incomes—over $20,000—are young men who look forward to being physicians, dentists, lawyers, and research scientists. Although any particular respondent may be overestimating or underestimating his ability, the group as a whole appears to be characterized by a reasonable degree of realism.

For about 4 out of 5 members of the group we have information about the locations in which they prefer to live and to work. Only 4 are so disturbed about the racial situation or about the relative lack of opportunities for Negroes in the United States that they expect to live abroad. One said: "I don't think I would like to live in the U.S. Being a Negro in a white hostile society does something to me. It makes me feel that I would not be capable of being a good father to a child if I lived here. I think I would make a better adjustment to fatherhood in a different social environment."

Another remarked: "I don't plan to live in the United States. I want new frontiers, like Brazil or Africa, and I intend to carry out these plans. I plan to work for some oil company and to forge ahead in some other country."

The picture of the group as a whole revealed a preference for the Northeast. About 1 out of 2 indicate this as the region of their first choice. These include about 80 percent of the Northerners and 16 percent of the Southerners. Here are some of the reasons why they prefer to live in this region:

"I would ideally like to live somewhere that's free of the vices and cruelties of the real world, but I have discovered that there is no ideal life. I would like to live in New York City, probably in an apartment."

"I'd like to live upstate or in New Jersey—somewhere away from police cars and policemen standing around reminding you that they're the law and you must obey."

"I like New York very much so I'd like to live here. I realized how much I liked New York when I was in the service in Virginia. I didn't make ties in the community and I didn't leave the post very often."

"I would like to live in the suburbs not too far from New York. I've lived in the South, but I would not want to raise children there because of racial tensions and the relative lack of educational opportunity."

"I'll probably not teach in New York. I like New England. I would like to live in a New England suburb and teach in some urban slum in Massachusetts."

"I don't intend to stay in Georgia. I have bad memories here but good memories of New England. I think I am a naturalist so the climate and the atmosphere there is a tremendous attraction. When I was there I felt more at home."

The second largest group expressed a preference for the South. It includes about 3 out of 5 Southerners and a very small number of Northerners:

"I think I'd like to stay here in Atlanta as far as I can see now. A lot of people say they live here because of the interracial harmony. My attitude is different from most Negroes. Where I want to live has nothing to do with race because my attitude at present is not developed as yet. I want to stay here because I feel my business would be better and the climate and the weather is moderate. The summers are lovely here. Knowing people my father worked on and their knowing me, I feel I would get a better start in my practice."

"I want to live in Atlanta because I've been living here for seventeen years. I've traveled a lot and I feel Atlanta is still where I want to live."

"I want to live in a small town, probably in the South. I just like the South. I visited all parts of the country except the Far West and I like the South best. Maybe because there's no place like home, but I don't like big cities."

"I feel I can accomplish my objectives or my aims in life by teaching in a Southern college, preferably an integrated college. I like the South better than the North."

Some are drawn to the South because it is home; others because it will be best for their work; and still others because they find that the tensions in a city like Atlanta are likely to be less than elsewhere. In short, the South continues to have a strong hold on many Negroes native to the area.

But a significant number of our Southerners—roughly 1 out of 5—and a smaller number of Northerners—roughly 1 out of 10—are drawn toward the West or Midwest. A Southerner who opts for the Midwest said: "I think I would like to live in the Midwest, maybe Iowa. Everything seems so calm and peaceful there.

Also, things will be more challenging in the North. People seem more aware and more interested in what goes on. People expect to go to see plays, to read, and to go to concerts. Exchange students from Iowa whom I have met bring the sense of going places. There seems to be a greater international influence there and a greater sense of cultural exchange, much richer experience than here. Here, things seem bogged down in tradition. People in the Midwest seem to be willing to consider different ideas."

Another is determined to get out of the South: "Definitely I would not like to live in the South or Southwest. It is stifling down here. The possible injustices and still poor communications between Negroes and whites are not at all attractive to me."

The matter of future location can also create considerable ambivalence: "I favor New York City because of the people, but I like the Southern climate and arboreal atmosphere. While I don't like the social attitudes of people in the South, I do like their greater warmth and demonstrativeness. I would not want my children to be in urban New York. On the other hand, suburbs foster reinstatement of the social past and conservatism. So, there is a dilemma about where to live."

But for the most part the problem did not create difficulties. Most of the Northerners looked forward to staying in the North and a somewhat smaller majority of Southerners wished to remain in the South. Only a minority looked forward to settling in the West.

Perhaps the most revealing finding with regard to this matter of future location is that so many Southerners do not look forward to "escaping" from the South. They do not consider the South to be oppressive. In fact, some believe that the level of racial tensions is lower there than elsewhere. It is difficult to say whether this acceptance of the South, which in many instances had the quality of affirmation, grows out of the adjustment of Southern Negroes to local conditions which makes the environment appear to be less oppressive; whether it reflects improvements in recent years in the elimination of gross forms of discrimination in the South; whether it bespeaks the sense of community and fellowship among particular Negro communities which compensate for deficiencies in white–Negro relationships; or whether middle-class Negroes cling to the status they have achieved, which is to a large extent dependent on local recognition. All these factors may be operative.

Among the most important decisions that a young man must make concerns marriage—whether to marry, when to marry, whom to marry, how many children to have, whether his wife should work, and what kind of family life he wants. We will begin our report of their family plans by quoting some general comments about marriage.

An older than average Northern college senior said: "I have been engaged and broke it off because I wasn't ready for it mentally. As I see it, the job I want (geographer in Africa) isn't conducive to marriage. In the social life I have, I have the pleasures of marriage. Marriage would be secondary to my plans and determinations."

One of the most cynical comments was the following: "I've thought about marrying a girl whom I really don't like as a means of avoiding military service. She just wants to be married. She's studying clinical psychology and we hate each other."

Another senior admitted that the idea of marriage is not easy for him to contemplate: "I find it difficult to picture myself as a married person. Frankly, I don't get along very well with the distaff side and this awareness detracts from involvement."

Several Southern high-school students see marriage as a burden which they want to postpone if not to escape: "I don't want to get married, too much responsibility for me. I don't want to ever marry. If I did the only reason would be to have a son. If I ever did get married, I would finish all my schooling first. I would want to practice medicine at least for a couple of years before I married. I am not basing my life on the way my family is now. I can't help thinking where I would be if I had three children and had to put all through college and had just bought a new house. Phew!"

Another put it thus: "I don't want to get married until I have reached my professional peak. I want to travel first before I get hog-tied. I want to travel by myself. Definitely and naturally family life means sacrifice and taking on new responsibilities."

But not every one felt this way. A Northern high-school student, aged seventeen, said: "I think I'd like to get married while I'm in college. I would like to get married right now. I feel marriage right now would be an aid in keeping my feet on the ground, but you can't get married without money or finances."

The pull toward early marriage, if for a different reason, is reflected in the following: "After law school I will marry, but I want to marry young because my father seems so much older than I am. He married late. I'd really like to marry in college but I can't afford to."

One view of how these young people feel about marriage can be obtained by considering the age at which they would like to marry. A very few want to marry before the age of twenty-one but the largest proportion, 55 percent, hope to marry between their twenty-first and twenty-fifth birthdays—that is, shortly after they are out of college. However, 30 percent do not want to marry until their late twenties, and over 10 percent want to wait till they are in their thirties.

Here are some brief comments about age at marriage:

"I don't think I would marry until after the M.S. Before that marriage might be an interference."

"I'd like to get married when I'm twenty-five. I think that's a realistic age in terms of my outlook on life, educational ambitions, financial condition and my sense of maturity."

"I would not get married until I'm about twenty-eight. I would be out of the service at twenty-five and I guess I'd need about three years to acquire security and assume responsibility."

A Northern sophomore said: "If I found the right girl who went along with my plans I'd marry about a year from now."

A Northern senior, aged twenty-two, remarked: "I would like to marry in about five years. I'm not ready now. I'm not emotionally ready now either."

Another Northern senior, aged twenty-one, indicated that he doesn't want to lose his freedom too early: "I think I would like to marry in my early thirties. I want to have a chance to live a little before then. I would hope that the girl I marry would be a real woman. Someone who knows how to please a man and also make a good mother. We would have to hit it off as I hate any aspect of phoniness."

The following remarks by seniors echo a great many replies: "I wouldn't consider getting married until I get established. I would like to have accumulated funds but that wouldn't be a condition for marriage." A Southern senior said: "I will wait until I get money in the bank and have security. I can't live off love. Two can't live off love. Two can't live as cheaply as one."

A large number of these young people are determined to get set in thir careers before they take on the burdens of marriage. Years ago most men from middle-class backgrounds felt the same way. Today, however, more and more young people are marrying early. Nevertheless, our group is responding to the ethos of an earlier day.

Only 2 young men in the entire group are already married and 5 report they are engaged. Apparently, what they say and what they are likely to do is congruent. Several of them stated that they need considerable time to figure out more carefully who they are and what they want. They also realize that the only basis on which they can get married and continue to study is to ask their parents to help support their wives—and this they are definitely disinclined to do.

But the vast majority contemplate marriage, sooner or later. What kind of girls do they think will make good wives? Pretty, sophisticated, independent, normal— these are some of the adjectives used to describe their ideal mates:

"Oh, I'd like a girl to be pretty. As my father says, 'Don't marry an ugly girl.' "

"Being a professional man I'll be looking for a wife with something in common with me who won't mind entertaining, who likes to be well-dressed, who has a sparkling personality, and who likes to meet people. In my profession I will want her to be always well-dressed."

"I'd like to marry, in December, a sophisticated, beautiful girl with good taste and a college degree."

Other young men are still a little uncertain: "I am not sure what woman it will be. I have got to support her. In cases like this, not the heart but the head must rule. She must be reasonable, intelligent and understanding, and sweet. She *must* be intelligent. It is O.K. to be intelligent. One can go to college and get a B.S. or Ph.D. and still not be intelligent. I want someone who can think.

Even if she only had a high-school education but could think, that would be O.K. I feel emphasis should be placed on the right thing, that is, her personality must be pure or close to it. She must love children."

One young man said: "I want to marry a normal girl, nothing like Sophia Loren, but I would have to love her." Another places stress on companionship: "She must be the sort of person I am, not a follower. She must take part and help me in everything I do. She must let me express myself, she must be a companion. She should know about what I'm doing. I know I would be a very devoted husband."

Many of them are quite specific about the level of education their prospective wives must have. Only 10 percent have no special preferences in this regard. Three-quarters of the remaining young men prefer wives with college or graduate degrees and only about 15 percent stated that high-school graduation alone would be sufficient. In short, a majority want wives who have achieved an educational level approximating their own.

Of those whose mothers are college graduates, 86 percent expect to marry women with a similar level of achievement, and there is no significant regional difference in this regard. None of the Southern young men whose mothers have less than a Bachelor's degree stipulated the same or less schooling for their wives, although a few said that educational achievement is irrelevant. In contrast, of the considerably larger group of Northerners whose mothers have had little or no college, somewhat less than half prefer to marry college graduates. The remaining youths will be satisfied to marry high-school graduates, or they have no educational qualifications for their future wives.

This is how some of the Southern men phrased their answers:

"I have a girl now who is in college. She is a freshman. I would much rather have a wife who is a college graduate. I would look for someone on my level of intelligence, class, and so forth. I believe that such marriages stay together longer. But I can't say definitely that I would marry only a college graduate."

"Of course she would have to be a college graduate."

"I would like her to have a B.S. or an A.B. degree. I figure like this: She must have knowledge in order to understand me, but as a doctor I could understand her very well."

"I am engaged to a young lady at Spelman. She will have her A.B. at the end of next year. I would like for her to have a Master's degree, if possible. That is, while I am continuing my studies, she can continue her studies."

Some Southerners take a more relaxed view and did not give much weight to formal education:

"I have not thought about her education for I feel education has nothing to do with love."

"I would want her to have a high-school education. I don't think more education is too important for a housewife. It is important for the man because he has to support a family."

"I feel love and schooling can't correlate. An intelligent person would not have to necessarily have a degree."

Similarly, there were many relaxed Northerners:

"I don't think college is really that important for girls and that would not be a deciding factor."

"I would stipulate that she have native intelligence rather than degrees."

"I would want her to have similar interests and have approximately the same or a similar education. But maybe that's not too important. How much I like her is probably more important."

"I'd want an intelligent girl but a higher education would not be critical. I would expect her to have an understanding and tolerant attitude."

Some Northerners attach special importance to their wives' having Bachelors' or graduate degrees:

"Ideally, I'd like an intelligent college girl with an advanced degree in chemistry but not higher achievements than mine. I would like her to be in the natural science field and that would include math."

"I'm more or less engaged—I plan to be married within two years, but I would not marry until I'm out of the service. The girl is smart, pretty, and fun to be with. She has a B.S. in Engineering (E.E. and math major) and will go into teaching at the grade-school or high-school level."

Several men explicitly stated that they do not want wives who are better educated or smarter than themselves:

"I would want her to have at least a high-school education but I would not want a woman who would outsmart me. But I would like her to be able to give me sound advice if I felt I had to discuss job changes or problems with someone who had my best interests at heart."

"I'd want a dependable trustworthy girl with a high-school education or more but not as much as I have. I would like to feel that I'm the head of the family."

How do these young men feel about their wives' working? One of the two married students has a wife who is currently working to help him complete his education: "I got married six months ago. She is a high-school graduate and works as a clerk for the American Express Company. She wants me to finish my education and is willing to support us while I go to school. Of course, I will help out with a part-time job."

The other husband sees no reason why his wife shouldn't work: "I married in the middle of my junior year. My wife was then a student at Spelman. Now she is taking a business course at a vocational school in Athens where she lives with my family. We expect a baby in three months. I have no special feelings about her working. Most families need a second income."

But there are many, approximately 1 in 5, who definitely prefer that their wives do not work:

"I know I think a woman's place is in the home. Mother rocks the cradle. My father preached that sermon yesterday in church."

"When we get married I want her to stay home. I feel

this way because when I was younger my mother worked and was away from home."

"I'd feel sort of bad if she had to work because I could not support a family."

There are a roughly equal number who think that they will prefer that their wives work:

"In most cases they should work because they need to meet more people. I get around and if she did she would not be stuck in the house all of the time. We would share the work in the house. She and I would both help."

"I want a girl who is interested in things, ambitious. I would prefer it if she had a career. The greatest happiness for an adult is in terms of a career and I would not want to deny this for her."

"As far as my wife's having a career and running a home, she could have both. I was raised in a situation where my mother held on to her career and I don't think there's anything drastically wrong with me."

Some gave answers based on the possibility of economic necessity:

"I would like her to have a career. I figure I would need a wife's financial help to maintain a family. If she didn't have a career we'd have to struggle. Her having a career could be the primary basis for marrying her as against someone else."

"I would not want her to work while we are married unless we needed the money. A woman's place is at home taking care of children and giving them love."

"I would marry a housewife. I would not want her to

work unless it was part time and only then to let her pay the gas bill just to remind her that, although the husband is the head of the house, the running of the house is not his full or exclusive responsibility."

Children, especially several children, were considered a block to a woman's working:

"If the family has more than one child I would not want her to work, but if we only had one I wouldn't mind. If she worked it would be easy to raise one child but not two or more because they wouldn't get enough attention."

"I would want her to work. In case there were any children, I guess she could stop working for a while."

"She would have to give up her career for the children. I don't want any neurotic babies running around the house. Children need parents."

The feelings of these young men run the full gamut including such elaborate formulations as:

"I would prefer that my wife stay home. I would prefer not to have her help out with the budget. American women, however, have to have a career so I suppose I could do nothing but let her do as she pleases about working."

"Well, if she really had to get out and work, after discouraging her I would let her work if she had character enough."

"I don't mind if she doesn't want to work, but I think it would be good for her if she does. I believe that a wife needs some wider interests."

"I would prefer that she didn't work. If she had a career I would try to discourage her and if I was unsuccessful I would try to go along with it."

It is interesting to see how the attitudes of these young men toward the possibility of their wives' working are related to the working status of their mothers. Somewhat more than half of the young men with working mothers have tolerant views toward their wives' work, while two-thirds of those whose mothers are at home prefer that their wives be homemakers. There are slightly more men who want their wives to follow the patterns of their mothers than the obverse, but the number who are willing to contemplate a different pattern is substantial. Few boys whose mothers have served as homemakers exclusively are dissatisfied with such concentration upon housekeeping and maternal responsibilities, and it is understandable that most of these wish their wives to emulate their mothers in this respect. Sons of working mothers, however, may have felt disadvantaged and this may be why more of them desire wives who will differ from their mothers in this.

We can summarize this discussion of the educational and work status of their future wives by saying that most of these young men want to marry women who share their interests, who have more or less similar educational backgrounds, and with whom they can look forward to planning their lives. They want companionship in marriage and they want their wives to be interesting persons. Of course, they want them to be good mothers.

How many children do these young men want to have? The most striking fact is that only a quarter want less than three children. Just under 40 percent have set three as their preference. But over a third want at least four children.

An example of one who wishes a small family is a Southern high-school boy: "At thirty I will be settled and married with one or two children—no more than three. The trouble today is that a lot of people raise large families. I have heard about a new program called Planned Parenthood, an effort to cut down on the number of people in the world. The life expectancy is long today and the death rate is small due to superior medical attention, so if people were to cut down on the number of children it would eliminate the problem of feeding so many. I personally believe in planned parenthood. I am not a member of a large family. I don't want to raise one. There was just my brother and me."

His viewpoint is supported by several Northerners:

"I want only one child. I am an only child and my mother was an only child. Opportunities are better if there is only one child since the parents can do more for this child as against three or four."

"I would stop at two children. Today's problem is that too many people are having too many children and can't support them."

But there are strong proponents of large families:

"I think I would like to have five children. I come from a small family and think that a large family is closer. My father came from a very large family, 18 children in all, and I have lots of cousins and I frequently wish that they were my brothers and sisters."

"I have three sisters and two brothers. I'd like at least six children myself. Yes, I have been influenced by my own family life. There is a greater bond between husband and wife."

"I'd like a large family—seven. I suppose because my family was small."

"I would like to have five or six children, both boys and girls. I feel it's essential for a couple to have children as they represent a binding and tempering force in a marriage."

In addition to the number of children, we find that many of the young men have quite explicit hopes about the sex of their children.

"Only wanting a son would cause me to marry. Seems to me you would have more worry about girls and pregnancy."

"I would like three children, two girls and a boy. Why two girls? I like girls and I want a boy to take my name."

"I would like to have three children—all boys. All boys because boys carry on the name."

"I would like two boys. Girls are more trouble."

"I'd like to have a large family of six or seven children with about four of them girls—I think little girls are very cute."

It is interesting that while one-quarter of these young

men would like to have families smaller than the one in which they grew up, half are looking forward to having larger families. Here indeed is strong affirmation of the future. In addition, these young men apparently anticipate realizing many important values from their immediate families.

We have learned that most of these young men look forward to having enough money to support their families adequately, if not in grand style. And several of them are planning to limit the size of their families to insure that they can give their children a good start in life.

Approximately half of the group look forward to making their homes in the suburbs which they believe are preferred environments for raising children: "I'd like to live in the South, as far out in Atlanta as possible, not cramped in with people. This is a better environment for rearing children and for my peace of mind. The schools tend to be better in the suburbs." Another remarked: "I would like to have a nice house and everything that goes along with it." A Northern student: "I would like to live in the suburbs as the more unsavory elements don't get a chance to move out into such a wholesome atmosphere." A Southerner: "I would want to live in a suburban area, peaceful and quiet. I like that."

Some see the future less in terms of family and children and more in terms of resolving problems with which they are currently struggling: "I would hope first of all to be at peace with myself, to be clear in my own mind about whom I'm obedient to, and to know clearly what I think is best for me. I want to live as fully as I can, to have an income that is sufficient for minimum living expenses. My dream is some time to have a big fireplace and a soft rug. I never really pictured the rest of the home. I never plan on sitting in an office or behind a desk, I'd be out where people are. I hope the world will be better by then."

And some are able to "think big": "I have a dream of starting a foundation out of earnings to give scholarships to boys who are above average but not superior. The superior boy will make a go of it anyway."

Others gave expression to what can be defined as the dream of the aspiring middle class:

"My father has a good life. I would like to have a life just like his, except he says that we children should do better. I want to have a comfortable home and three or four children and a good family life. To be secure and happy is most important."

"Ten years from now I would like to have a good job and a growing family. I'd like to be making $800 a month and belong to a country club if there is one."

"I plan to be a doctor who wants to be part of the community. I am interested in people and will take part in civic organizations. I could participate and help in more ways than one. Our white brothers have had and done this long ago. I plan to be this type of individual."

Travel and children are linked in several of the young men's comments:

"When I do have spare time on a Saturday or on a

Sunday, I'll probably read a lot on my occupation. I'll take up some sports like golf or tennis or bowling for relaxation. Then I would sit around and raise the kids right and be henpecked. I'll help my wife with the dishes and travel with my family because I know I would be without them a lot in my travels on the job. I would have to give time to the family whenever I had the chance."

"I would like to travel and to be well informed and to participate in governmental affairs. I like to voice my opinions, whatever they are. Everyone must be a voter. Of course, I enjoy going to parties and dances and I like going to concerts and I enjoy family group activities. I would hope to have a wholesome relationship with my children if I have any."

"I would spend my leisure with my children. I believe a family should be close. We would go hunting and fishing and have a good time. In my leisure time I would also try to acquaint myself with the newest technology and methods in my profession of medicine."

Family and school have apparently done their work well. These are young people with broadening horizons who see their future in terms of what they can make of themselves and how they can provide secure foundations for strong family units. They hope to derive pleasure and satisfaction from their wives with whom they look forward to sharing life's excitement and troubles; they seek satisfactions in raising children. Yet, as much as they anticipate the pleasures associated with marriage and fatherhood, they are realistic enough to know that these will be better carried out under conditions of maturity and financial security. Therefore, they do not expect to embark upon them before they reach positions in the work world that provide them with the wherewithal to realize their ambitions.

They envision incomes sufficient to enable them to live comfortably and they do not believe it will be necessary to rely upon the earnings of their wives. They are somewhat conservative about their wives' working; this may reflect their knowledge that for so long most Negro women had to work, married or not, and often they were the chief support of their families. They want no part of that old pattern. They want to be the heads of their households.

Most of them plan to live where they were born and raised, but some of the Southerners plan to live in regions where they will be less inhibited because of their race. Almost without exception they look forward to being residents of large metropolitan centers. Some prefer the city proper; most prefer the suburbs. Many look forward to travel as a way to broaden their horizons and those of their children.

The expectation of these young men about the lives they hope to lead is little different from the anticipations of college students in the white community. They want much the same things that other young Americans with similar backgrounds desire. Their goals have not been conditioned by their race as much as by their family background and educational achievements. And these have given them every confidence that they can function as respectable and respected members of the community.

7: EQUALITY OF OPPORTUNITY

If the goals of middle-class Negro youths are conditioned primarily by their background and education rather than by the factor of color, as these young men have indicated, this decreased concern about their race is a recent phenomenon. As we have noted, it is only since World War II that changing attitudes and practices in the United States have permitted young Negroes such as these to base their plans for the future upon their own desires and talents with little reference to their racial identity.

Although a variety of circumstances have led to the recent changes in race relations, much of the success that has been achieved in moving the Negro's position closer to that of other members of the American community is the result of the activities of the Civil Rights movement. It was not until the Negro community itself began to agitate for reforms and, by dramatizing its plight, to arouse the conscience of white Americans that the inch-by-inch progress of the postwar period developed into long strides.

Since Civil Rights activity is directed toward a fundamental alteration of the relations of the Negro to

American society, it would appear that no Negro can be indifferent to the struggle or to the outcome. Few Negroes do not know instinctively that the success of their protest will materially affect their futures and the futures of their children.

To most young men in this study, the impact of the Civil Rights movement upon their present and future lives is an acknowledged fact. Many interviewees indicated they are well aware that their sanguine approach to the future is in large part due to the achievements of the Civil Rights movement. Yet they exhibited a variety of attitudes about different aspects of the movement and varying degrees of involvement in it. As we might have surmised, the overwhelming reaction of the young people toward the Civil Rights movement is strongly positive despite critical comments about its leadership, tactics, and concerns.

Among those who expressed unqualified approval is the Southern high-school senior who said: "I am for Civil Rights, not against, no, no. I'm no Uncle Tom. I want either my rights or death. . . . They are God's rights and my very existence and I should not have to go out and get my head beat by someone who doesn't want to give me my rights." A Northern student stated: "The Civil Rights movement is one of the best things that ever happened to Negroes."

Yet a few boys expressed indifference. A Southern sophomore who is an aspiring musician said: "I am not excited about the Civil Rights movement. I think that we've become complacent. The key to opportunity lies in accepting opportunities and responsibilities and in education." A Southern high-school senior stated: "I am not quite interested. I have read about Reverend King and others and I believe in betterment for all people. I am concerned about my race but they are going ahead now and I intend to help the whole human race and not just Negroes." A classmate asserted: "There is nothing in race relations that upsets me. I am not interested in how the country is run. Let them run it. I am a Theosophist. That is, I believe in the supremacy of God. Whatever will be, will be."

A Southern college senior said: "I don't allow myself to think about the Civil Rights movement. I'm going back to my childhood rearing; I'm trying to love my brothers, black or white." A classmate admitted: "I am more or less lukewarm. I have not been totally anti-white or pro-Negro. I am not the angry young Negro. I have not been affected too much personally. I have really been encouraged to exert my full capacity as a Negro. I am not unaware of injustices. But I have a moderate or tolerant attitude toward the white person and toward these changes."

While these boys show a lack of concern they do not actively disapprove of the goals of the Civil Rights movement. No intelligent person does. However, several who acknowledge the need for improvement in the Negroes' conditions have various reservations about the nature of the protest. Some boys express theoretical objections while others confine their criticisms to certain specific aspects of the movement.

Among the most severe critics is a Northern senior who said: "I think the Negroes should do more for themselves instead of emphasizing the mass approach. I feel I'm furthering the Negro cause by putting myself ahead. Negroes should be more concerned with personal development." Another thinks: "The Civil Rights movement does not demand enough for the Negro. Social equality and pushing for equal rights are not enough. What's wrong is that there is a lack of internal movement within the race." Another classmate remarked: "I'm pessimistic about progress in the Civil Rights movement. Prejudice in whites runs deep since whites have a difficulty in identifying with Negroes. In the South it was only when a white minister and woman were killed that the local whites could identify with the victims. I am more interested in political action than Civil Rights."

Although there are more Southern youths who were neutral about the movement than Northerners, more Southerners, expecially college youth, reported participating in Civil Rights activities. But both Southerners and Northerners had considerable criticism about strategy and tactics.

A Northern high-school senior approves of the movement but thinks that "it infringes on personal liberties if you're not able to use your property as you see fit." A Northern college senior feels that "the emphasis should be in terms of individuals being helped by groups rather than a mass approach and demonstration." Another senior said: "The root of the Negro problem is not being dealt with. There should be more emphasis at the level of the individual family. Superficial planning and projects lead only to nonsignificant and superficial changes in living conditions. The Negro needs to be helped to realize his potential thereby stretching his potential and increasing his challenges. This would be one way of getting him out of his psychological morass."

Some of these boys deplore the lack of participation by the middle-class Negro. For example, a Northern senior remarked: "Those who can contribute don't contribute, such as college-educated Negroes who could do voluntary work and take an active part in the movement." A Southern sophomore noted: "Teachers were reluctant to help in the Civil Rights movement but the best teachers did." A Northern sophomore said: "The middle-class Negro is motivated to get away from the problems which lower-class Negroes face, and it's hard for middle-class Negroes to get angry and demonstrate. They're too comfortable." A classmate thinks: "There is a need for a greater 'help my brother' attitude among middle-class Negroes."

Some students think that Negro participation in general is not as substantial as it should be. A Southern sophomore feels: "White college students use the Civil Rights movement to register generalized rebellion rather than genuine interest in Negro civil rights. This makes for phonies in the Civil Rights movement and brings out a false militancy which cannot be sustained. White students are not able to participate genuinely and, on the other hand, Negro students are not sufficiently involved." A Northern college senior would like to see "the Negro become a more active participant in his own enfranchisement and more interested in the quality of his own life. I don't think the Civil Rights movement demands enough from the Negro."

A few others made remarks about the possible participation of other groups. A Northern sophomore thinks: "The Catholic Church should participate. . . . They're always preaching brotherly love and not doing anything active to help Negroes. They are a powerful social force and could help Negroes by influencing whites." Another sophomore thinks that "more Northern whites should be involved in helping Northern Negroes." A Northern senior suggested that "there should be more involvement of Negro professionals and lower elements." Another would like to see "more political involvement of Northern Negroes such as was demonstrated in the Mississippi group of doctors and nurses."

The tactics utilized by various Civil Rights groups also elicited many remarks. A Northern senior advocates "a more militant stand along lines of sheer force or economic boycott rather than appeals for patience." Another senior said: "I take a dim view of marches. Concentration should be on the economic and educational uplift of the Negro." A Northern high-school senior asserted: "The Civil Rights movement is not being carried out in an orderly fashion. People get hurt and people get killed. The demonstrations should be more orderly and less wild. I didn't go for those riots and no one should feel afraid to walk in Harlem." A classmate said: "I don't believe violence serves a constructive purpose and I don't feel young children should be bussed out of their neighborhoods."

A Southern high-school senior, on the other hand, protested: "I am violently opposed to nonviolence. You have to retaliate. I would rather knock my brains out trying to get something that is mine. I had a friend once who said he was for a nonviolence movement, but if someone hit his girl friend his reaction would be different." A Southern sophomore believes that "Negroes in the South should be armed (via the Deacons movement) to protect themselves from the Ku Klux Klan."

Critics of Civil Rights leadership include a Northern sophomore who considers Martin Luther King "too proud and evangelistic to be a national leader or politician since his point of view is not motivated by the rational facts or by the actual issues but by his orientation to God. Malcolm X has my respect. I like his approach of direct analyses of social and economic issues." Another sophomore said: "Roy Wilkins bugs me sometimes because he is too laden with white values. I like the former head of CORE, James Farmer."

A Northern high-school boy scored "conflicts among the top leaders. Some are not as active organizationally and adept as they should be." A Northern college senior thinks: "Martin Luther King has done an admirable job in the South. In the North, I'm critical of the white leadership of the Civil Rights movement. For example, Adam Clayton Powell in New York has sat back and done practically nothing. The same thing applies to Dawson of Chicago. They have not led Negroes, and neither have they set a participation example that might inspire other Negroes. I think Negroes who are politically prominent have a strategic value in the Civil Rights movement. They have let the Negro people down." Another senior remarked: "If James Baldwin headed up a Civil Rights organization I'd join right now because I see him as the most realistic person in terms of social perception and social action. He has a good perception of what's happening but possibly not why its happening."

Some youths have strong opinions about the effectiveness of various organizations in the movement. A Northern senior said: "The Black Muslim movement is an anachronism. It would have been timely after the Civil War." Another senior asserted: "I'm against CORE. It's a radical group of Jewish people. The NAACP is ineffectual because it doesn't stimulate youths to be active. HARYOU is a farce. I went down there to donate my services and they could not even give me a brochure. The NAACP students here at CCNY drink sodas and gossip." A Northerner said that he doesn't like SNCC "because of the radical minded people associated with it and the radicalism which evolves." On the other hand, one of his classmates said: "I believe that groups should be active but I don't like CORE because CORE is too militant and its tactics are untactful. I favor the NAACP because it has a good record of solid achievements, and SNCC because it is a youth movement led by astute leaders."

This is what these young people told us about their participation in the movement. One Southern sophomore reported: "I was a member of the Atlanta Committee on Appeal for Human Rights during high school. I worked part time for SNCC while I was a college student before I took a full-time job on a leave of absence basis to go to Americus." He has now returned to Morehouse on a SNCC scholarship. A classmate said: "I served as acting president of the Youth Council (in Ocala, Fla.) until I went to college. I went to classes all the morning and demonstrated all the afternoon. I was in jail several times."

A Southern senior related the following event: "I went to the Crystal chain stores and sat down at the counter and was refused service. The waitress called the cops and when they got there she said we had pushed her around. Imagine that! She was on the other side of the counter! We were fined $200 and placed on one year of probation."

A Northern high-school student reported: "I belong to the NAACP and I am considering joining CORE because CORE is more progressive." A Northern college senior said: "I like to think of myself as a fairly active participant. I helped organize students into the Afro-American Society."

What about those who did not participate? What reasons do they give? In general, nonparticipation has been due to personal inhibitions or to disinterest. For example, a Northern sophomore admitted: "I have wanted to go picketing and haven't, and it's not because I'm not interested but because I'm a little shy. I hope to get over that." A Northern senior said: "I couldn't do that—parade around. I could not march. I'd feel very uncomfortable." A Northern high-school senior supposed: "I'm the type that likes to sit back and let the other guy do all the work." A Southern college senior said: "I believe certain people are cut out for the movement like Martin Luther King. I am not this type of person. I would rather be in my lab doing research work."

Disinterest was explained by a Northern sophomore: "Right now I have neither the desire nor the time for active or organizational participation." A Northern high-school senior admitted: "I don't feel any involvement in the securing of rights but I'm all for it." A classmate remarked: "I have never thought about participating in it myself."

A few boys believe that involvement in Civil Rights activities might jeopardize their schooling. A Southern sophomore who was active in such a movement in high school stated: "I have not been keeping up with the

Civil Rights movement. I intend to finish college and I don't find it necessary to go to jail. This would hamper my progress in college." A Southern college senior said that he participated only to a minimum extent: "I did not get really involved because most who did neglected their studies. And in the long run it became very damaging to them. But I have not."

Some boys were discouraged from participation by their parents. A Northern high-school sophomore said: "My mother told me not to get involved in picketing." A Northern college senior stated: "My parents, because of economic and social fear, would not permit me to participate but I feel sacrifices have to be made to foster programs." A Southern college senior said: "I have not been a sit-in and have no jail sentence. My parents discouraged me from getting a record."

A few youths deplore their lack of opportunity to engage in demonstrations. A Southern college senior volunteered: "I really haven't done anything in the field of Civil Rights. I guess I was not at the right place at the right time. When I was at De Pauw, there was no movement up there because, really, there were not enough Negroes in the school. I then went to Talledega but there was an injunction against students. We couldn't march. We could not be violent. If you decided to get out of school you could do these things. However, this would have hindered me in my program."

In evaluating the effect of the Civil Rights movement,

some talked about what it meant to them personally and others reflected on its larger impact on Negroes and American society. A few dealt with both aspects.

Some discussed Civil Rights in terms of what it had done for their self-image. A Southern college senior said: "I have a self-awareness and sense of dignity. Probably we all had this but had not recognized it, but now it is recognized and we do have a sense of belonging." A classmate agrees: "I have always had reservations about how I would fit in. It is definitely helping me to form a new image of myself in the white community." Still another said: "I find I have more confidence within me. I don't have to worry about myself. I feel more confident that I am a part of this country, so that there is nothing to fear."

A Southern high-school senior noted: "One thing, it makes you feel better as an individual. I guess the word to use is 'accepted.' " A classmate said: "Civil Rights has changed my life a lot. Now, there is no difference regardless of color or creed. Sometimes, I would say I wish I were white, but I don't think like that now. If you were born a certain color you should not put your head down but hold it up."

Some boys spoke about social advantages accruing from the Civil Rights movement. A Southern high-school senior related: "When I was younger I went to a Crystal store and was asked out. I remember about the back door at the Fox. We go into the front door now, you know. Now, all the kids, white and colored, socialize together at places of recreation. I have regular white associates at places that I go to play golf." One of his classmates said: "The good things about Civil Rights now are that I can go places where I could not go at one time and I can eat at restaurants and enjoy the many luxuries that other people enjoy."

A few stated specifically that they can see no personal effects from the Civil Rights movement. A Southern sophomore who is entering the field of music said: "I can't believe that Civil Rights will make any essential difference in my future. Anybody who wants to achieve can and I don't think my being a Negro has any effect at all."

However, the great majority of those who commented on the personal effects of the Civil Rights movement tend to feel that it has made a difference, although not quite as much as the Southern high-school student who said: "Civil Rights has changed my life a lot. The advantages we have gained by sit-ins have helped in that there is no difference regardless of color or creed."

This is how some of these young people assessed the broader implication of the Civil Rights movement. They see it as making a major contribution toward assuring the Negro his rightful place in American democracy. No longer will color be the determining factor. As a Northern high-school senior remarked: "It will give the white people in the South an opportunity to understand Negroes through more contact and then they'll find there's no difference."

But optimistic as they are, many have reservations about the speed of the transformation. A Southern sophomore said, "I think the Civil Rights movement will have made some significant differences in the sense that people in the country as a whole are more aware of the meaning of the concepts of democracy and equality. I believe we can regulate behavior but I don't believe that we can legislate morality. Perhaps we can get to the place when laws can influence people's attitudes toward other people by helping to create situations in which it's possible for their relationships to change. I don't believe, though, that this is enough to influence how people really feel toward other people." A Southern senior commented: "The public mind is on the injustices heaped on the Negro. This has helped. What I am wondering is how long this will last. The Civil Rights movement has made them aware of conditions. But I'm skeptical about how long this movement will have the sympathy of the public."

Some spoke of the effects on Negroes personally. A Northern senior thinks: "The Civil Rights movement gives the Negro an opportunity to discover and rediscover his personality. There are cultural and individual implications. The Northern Negro has now discovered his African background and, in general, the Rights movement has made possible the reaffirmation of the Negro." A classmate said: "The main thing that has come out of it is a feeling of racial pride. Once a man gets that, anything is possible." A Southern senior believed that "the Civil Rights movement has made the Negro more aware of his plight."

Some young men single out particular groups of Negroes who are likely to benefit more from the current efforts. A Southern college sophomore said: "The lot of the middle-class Negro is better. The lower-class Negro just doesn't care that much about where and what he is. He thinks it's a lot of fuss about nothing. The lower-class Negro really doesn't know and doesn't care what's going on." A Northern sophomore stated: "Martin Luther King has done a fantastic job with Southern Negroes in bringing them nearer the level of Northern Negroes. But he can't do much for Northern Negroes. The Northern Negro has higher economic status. The black bourgeoisie has too many false values."

Reflecting on the long-range impact of Civil Rights, a Northern sophomore remarked: "In another generation Negroes will present a threat to the white economic structure. Also, other minorities will come into their own while Negroes become more conservative." A classmate forecast: "In twenty-five years, the situation might get worse in the North because of the crime rate and Negro–white hostility which may break out in open violence —like the riots." Another Northern sophomore said: "In twenty-five years there will probably be more political power among Negroes in the South than the North but the large cities will probably have Negro mayors."

A Northern college senior believes, as do many others, that "in twenty-five years there will be a great improvement in racial feelings. The critical area is that of feelings—they change the slowest." A classmate would like to see "a completely independent power base similar to what Malcolm X had in mind and headed up by a national figure such as Martin Luther King or Adam Clayton Powell. There should be more Negro leaders in positions of independent power so that the demands of the Negro people can be properly voiced. I would also expect a greater acceptance of citizenship. Negro middle-class power is based on wanting to identify with the white middle class and as such, they become more conservative. I also think people's feelings change slowly, but do change." Another Northern senior thinks: "Progress will depend on the degree of acceptance that whites will have for Negroes and Negro aspirations, but this factor may be offset by the increasing economic and political strength of Negroes. Prejudice will change more slowly than discrimination and there will probably always be a lag between feelings and laws."

A Southern high-school senior said. "Civil Rights is the law which might open things up but will not change people. People will be the same; there will be some nice and polite white people, but socially they will say things like, 'I don't want to let my girl go out with that nigger.' I don't completely trust them." A Southern college senior approves of the Civil Rights movement but thinks: "It came late. It should have come twenty-five or thirty years ago. Only the middle-class Negro can carry out the program demanded by the opening up of jobs. In the next generation there should be a step-up of the program in the courthouse but not in the streets."

A Northern high-school senior summed up the sentiments of most of these boys: "In a number of years, I don't know how many, we'll be on an equal level. But we'll still have to deal with feelings of racial hatred and discrimination. I don't know how this problem can be dealt with since your thoughts can't be controlled by anyone else."

Civil Rights activity has been motivated by the need to provide the Negro American with the same possibilities for personal fulfillment as the white American has enjoyed. However, while the Negro has never been an equal member of the American community, he has always been an integral part of it. This has meant that he shares with the white population a national identity, although not a racial identity. When certain developments have a national impact, both Negro and white partake of whatever benefits or suffer whatever misfortunes ensue. Thus, while the Negro has been concentrating his efforts upon improving the conditions of his own group, he is not unaware that such comprehensive circumstances as war, technological change, or economic growth can have an even more determining effect on the shape of his life.

For the young men in our group, the hostilities in Vietnam with the prospect of the draft represent such a circumstance. These young men tend to respond to the draft in much the same way as their white confreres—a few see military service as an opportunity, more consider it a waste of time; a few are violently opposed to serving, most are willing to serve, if drafted, but preferably after their studies are completed.

Among those who are strongly opposed to military service is a Northern college senior: "School is saving me. I would like to avoid military service by getting tied up with an industrial job that is halfway vital. I don't want to go into the service. First it would be a waste. I know some fellows who were shipped down South and they could not go to school. I am not inclined to put on a uniform and begin fighting for the U.S. What would I be fighting for? I'd feel like a prize jackass out on a field with a rifle. What would I be fighting to maintain? My brother was in the Marines for nine years and it didn't do anything for him."

Only a little less hostile is another Northern college senior: "I have a negative attitude toward the military in general. I am not a pacifist but I'm against war and war plans. I'm against R.O.T.C. on a liberal arts campus. I'm against the spending of money for military purposes. If I received a notice to report I'd report, but I'd go in with a bad attitude. If I could, I would exercise the alternative of remaining in New York in intelligence. An assignment to Kansas would be the same as one in Vietnam. Killing Vietnamese would be the same as taking orders from a sergeant in Kansas. I participated in anti-war demonstrations, signed petitions, and carried placards. My parents agree in principle with my stand but are aghast that I would go if called. If I had to go now I would consider it an interruption to my studies. I also believe that college students are unjustly favored over others."

Another negative view was formulated by a Northern sophomore: "I would not resist going in but I would not choose to go in. As far as I'm concerned, those two years would be a waste of time, and it is an activity which imposes a deterioration of the intelligence. As far as physical benefits are concerned, I do my physical build-up by myself—I go to a gym on the weekends. Part of my aversion to military service is related to this country's tendency of taking over and holding down local development in foreign lands. The U.S. commercializes—the marketing of Pepsi Cola is an example."

A Southern sophomore is a conscientious objector: "I believe the draft is wrong and I am a conscientious objector. I have appealed for a C.O. status. I can't believe there is any such thing as for God *and* country; it's God *or* country." And another Southerner, a high-school senior: "I don't want to go into the service, no, I want to avoid it completely. I don't even want to think of it."

At the opposite extreme are several young men who have a positive orientation toward the services:

"I will go into the Air Force immediately upon graduation in 1967. Not because of my brother but because of the service itself—I like it. There's more mobility in the Air Force. I would like to fly or navigate. I'll take the courses which I think would be of help to me. The AAF could possibly turn into a career, but I haven't given it any serious thought. I also like the chance for travel that the AAF offers."

"I like the Marines. You go in a boy and you come out a man. They treat you stern. But in the Air Force there would be more than a chance of going overseas. It's a change. I have never been further than Massachusetts and that's no change at all."

"I prefer the Navy. This branch offers more advantages. There are a wide variety of occupations you can choose from. I signed up when I was eighteen. I will get the advantages of the G.I. Bill which will help me to go to school."

"If I don't go to college my second choice would be to go into the Air Force and there I would major in electronics. I went to the various branches and found that in the Air Force I would get a better opportunity to go to school. I would want the best program if I didn't go to college. I would have to reenlist, however, for another two years in order to have funds enough to go back to college. I could pay the Air Force back by working here in Atlanta."

The most typical position was a willingness to serve if drafted, after completing school:

"I have thought about the military service but try to keep it out of my mind as much as possible. I know I won't be drafted while I am in college. I wouldn't consider military service as a career. If there was a danger of the draft I would enlist in the Air Force rather than the Army. My hobby used to be building model planes and I think I would like it better, surely better than the Army."

Almost half of the young men who express a choice of service prefer the Air Force. The next most popular service is the Army, selected by 1 out of 4. Among the Southerners, however, the Army is in last place. The Marines are more popular with high-school than with college men. The popularity of the Air Force appears to result from a belief that it is less military, offers more opportunities for skill acquisition, and offers more equal opportunities to Negroes.

Although only a rare young man considers that widespread discrimination of Negroes is grounds for refusal to serve in the armed forces, we must be cautious when we make inferences from their resigned acceptance of the obligations of military service. After all, few men, black or white, are eager to enter the military forces, particularly in times of armed conflict, but fewer still are willing to suffer the punishment imposed for refusal to serve. Certainly these young men have affection for their native land, and Negroes have served in all of this nation's wars despite their subjugation by the majority race. Their continued willingness to serve hardly denotes a new surge of patriotism allied to Civil Rights accomplishments. But, as Negroes who can expect to reap the most immediate benefits from the racial revolution, these young men will support the country that is supporting them in their struggles for equality. Also, they recognize that recent changes in the armed forces should permit them to have equal access to positions commensurate with their abilities.

In general, then, these youths are highly realistic about the future course of events for the Negro. They have confidence in themselves because of the special advantages they have had, but they believe that it will be a long time before their opportunities will spread to the less fortunate Negro. Above all, although they tend to think that increased interracial contacts will benefit Negroes, they know that prejudice cannot be quickly eradicated.

They are sophisticated and articulate in their evaluation and criticisms of the Civil Rights movement. While some of them are highly critical, they may be reflecting the frustrations of youth. Many of them have developed a cynicism and alienation from the Negro leadership. Yet, although they believe that the search for equality will be a task that will take many years, few doubt that it will eventually be achieved.

8: THE IMPACT OF RACE

Although the preceding material indicates that the matter of race does not dominate the plans and aspirations of these young men, they are hardly unconcerned with the fact that they are Negroes in a predominately white society. We have already reported their opinions about the progress and prospects of the Civil Rights movement as it affects their own lives and the lives of fellow Negroes. We shall now consider their attitudes toward the matter of race in general and as it specifically affects their goals. Thus, we shall obtain some idea of the new worlds that they think are within their grasp, and of the obstacles they may have to surmount to reach them.

A few of the young men actually see their race as an asset in the pursuit of their goals. This view is set forth clearly by a Southern college senior: "It is an advantage for me to be a Negro. So many white people probably have guilty consciences that they bend over backwards to be liberal and this evidences itself in terms of scholarships for Negroes."

A similar statement, unmodified by the awareness of special pressures, is made by another Southern senior from a neighboring institution: "In the past there were obstacles to being a member of my race, but today one of the greatest assets is to be a Negro. The only difference that being a Negro will make is to make one more aware of the necessity to do a good job."

One Southern high-school senior ascribes his good fortune in earning a scholarship to Yale specifically to the fact that he is a Negro. He makes some interesting observations about color: "I believe Yale accepted me because I am a Negro. If I were darker, they would like it more. I don't believe in color; there are advantages to pass for white. I'm pleased with my complexion. I don't want to be darker unless I were a pretty color like the Negroes in Ebony. I am not color-conscious. I would like a pretty brown wife but she must have good hair. White girls don't interest me. They are repulsive." He is more than a little "color conscious."

More of them consider being a Negro not as an asset but as a liability, both because of the burdens of the past and because of the way power and influence are still largely in the hands of the white population. A Southern senior reads the lessons of history: "You see, Negroes have not been in the privileged class for a length of time, so we do not trust ourselves and we do not trust our children to handle money wisely. The Jews have trusted their children for a long time. If the child is to master both education and culture, he must have known these things or had them for a long time. It is only recently that Negroes have had a good life, and we have not learned to trust ourselves or our children."

The handicaps which result from social and cultural segregation are stressed by a sophomore: "If I were not Negro I would have had more experience. In the small town where I grew up a white child would be told about the concerts and be urged to go. I could read about them, but experience is much better. I would have been exposed to a different value system on the basis of wider experience."

An explanation of the subtle difficulties which face Negroes in competing with whites was formulated by a perceptive college senior: "Unfortunately, the whites have responsible jobs in business. There are a greater number of white applicants than Negroes who are qualified and interested who also want these jobs and who are familiar with these jobs through their families. The question of recommendations comes in too, and I do not know anyone with influence, so my recommendations may not have the impact of theirs."

Several young men believe that they will be stimulated by having to compete with the more influential and firmly entrenched whites: "Sometimes I would say, 'I wish I were white,' but I don't think like that now, because if you were born a certain color you should not put your head down but hold it up. I will make it, I believe. I will make money and, in time, by hard work, I will do things better because I am a Negro and have white competition. This competiton will not stop me but only make me work harder for the future."

Another Southerner said: "Last summer I went to the

University of North Carolina and there lived in a dormitory. For a few weeks the students would not even speak to me, but the first test showed that I was far above them. I remained at the top of the class and they changed their opinion of me and they all became very pleasant."

A few young men have thought about what life might be like if they were white, but these reflections served only to arouse anxiety: "I've thought about how it would be if I were not a Negro and it frightens me. I would probably be just what I am now. I wouldn't want to be a person who hates other people." Again: "I've never given any thought to what life would be like if I were not a Negro until the last two years. I have two roommates who are very light colored and very color conscious and they talk a great deal about how better things would be if they were not Negroes."

Apart from personal differences and some of the differences are substantial, all of these young men indicate attitudes toward race which explicitly or implicitly express the hope and expectation that an individual soon will be accepted for his intrinsic value and that all individuals will be able to accept themselves. But as we have seen in our discussion of Civil Rights, many feel that this time will be far in the future.

One reliable touchstone of how students feel about the role of race in their lives is the way they assess the issue in making career choices and, second, in their planning for education, military service and future residence.

The most striking fact is the considerable number of the total group who did not make any mention of matters of race in discussing their occupational plans. This silence could be interpreted to mean that race is such an overwhelming reality that many young Negroes see no need to make it explicit, particularly when discussing it with other Negroes. But this interpretation may not be entirely valid since the majority of those who did deal explicitly with considerations of race in discussing their occupational choice did not see it as a special burden or deterrent.

Here are some of the young men who see broadened opportunities open to them as Negroes. A Northern high school senior said that there are now "employment opportunities and promotions in engineering because of the Civil Rights movement." A Southern college sophomore stated: "Many industries are opening up for Negroes. It will be fairly easy to go into space engineering." A Southern high-school senior expects "to be an architectural apprentice in a white firm. Race would not affect me."

Several respondents asserted that ability is now more important than race or even that racial considerations are completely irrelevant to their plans. These included a Northern sophomore who thinks: "Being a Negro doesn't constitute a career hazard any more," and one of his Southern counterparts who believes: "The level I am aiming for (in law) will be governed more by individual ability than by artificial restrictions." A Southern senior hopes: "Being a Negro will not hinder me. Individual ability is the most important factor." And an Atlanta high-school student claimed: "Civil Rights showed me I could go higher than I plan. If you are ambitious no one can stop you."

A few related their aspirations to the needs of the Negro community. A Morehouse sophomore from Mississippi said: "We always heard that there was a great need for Negro lawyers and I understand that there are not too many Negro lawyers who go into politics." A Southern college senior noted: "There are only a few Negro physicians in research and specialties but there are many new opportunities. I'll contribute to history as a Negro should."

Others recognize that discriminatory practices do exist among either employers or consumers of services but are sanguine about their ability to overcome these obstacles and to gain access to employment in integrated situations. A Southern senior, aiming for a medical career, believes that the "attitudes about Negro doctors are changing among both white and Negroes," both of whom "had little regard for Negro doctors in the past." A Southern sophomore wants a job handling legal contracts for a large corporation: "There are not many such openings for Negroes but I can do it if I'm well prepared." A Southern senior noted: "Race still is a factor but we have better opportunities than before."

Some noted preferential hiring of Negroes and envision being in advantageous positions relative to whites. For example, a Southern senior thinks: "It might be comparatively easier for me to get a job than for a white person of similar or better background"; and a Southern sophomore stated: "Companies are actually looking for Negro research chemists." A Southern senior who aspires to high governmental office thinks: "Race might be an asset in politics, rather than a handicap."

Not all of the young men see their occupational future as quite so comfortable. Several continue to believe that their being Negro will prove to be a handicap. A Northern sophomore, for example, "thought about being a chemical engineer but wondered about placement as a Negro." He switched to accounting and envisions working for the government which "provides a better chance for fair competition." A Southern college senior feels: "I must be better than the average white person and my credentials must be higher."

A few youths are concerned about the availability of career opportunities for Negroes. A Southern high-school student believes: "There are no large Negro corporations to afford me an occupation, but later white friends might hire me or there may be more Negro businesses which will need my services." A Northern high-school senior said he was warned that "only five Negro boys have made it in pharmacy up to now." However, he plans to make the attempt.

In addition to considerations of race in these young men's assessment of their occupational future, the issue was also a concern in the planning of some of the group with respect to their future location, education, and military service. Those who plan to throw in their lot with the Negro community, North or South, look forward to living in Harlem or in some part of the Southern Black Belt. A Southern sophomore from Evansville, Indiana, plans to return there because he "understands there are many openings for Negroes in business." A Northern high-school student thinks: "California is good or better for Negro professionals than it is here."

A large number who look forward to attending college or graduate school concern themselves with matters of race in evaluating alternative institutions. There was, for instance, the Southern college sophomore who stated: "Most schools which today are open to Negroes weren't open to my father." A classmate noted that he was "the first Negro to enter Ocala Junior College [which he had attended prior to going to Morehouse]. I had to show them I was as good as they were." Another sophomore who wants to study dentistry said: "We have a better chance to get an education. I want to go to Alabama where the education is better." A Southern senior will be the first Negro at the University of Florida Medical School. "I hope I am hardened to prejudice," he remarked. A Southern sophomore "might even go to law school at the University of Mississippi. There's a good chance I may be enrolled there." A Southern sophomore said: "It is very possible that I will fit into a white university. Students are not necessarily prejudiced, nor are the professors." A Southern high-school student said: "I originally selected Clark but now I find it easier to talk with people of other races, so I've changed to Georgia Tech."

Another way in which race plays a part in their considerations relates to the question of scholarships and fellowships. A Southern senior said that the availability of scholarship aid makes it "an advantage for me to be a Negro." Two Northern high-school seniors expect to receive support from the National Negro Scholarship Fund, and a Southern sophomore, looking forward to law school, said: "I may go to Harvard, possibly, because Morehouse students get many grants from there."

But not all of our young men are willing to venture forth into the white world. A minority continues to have reservations, largely on social grounds. A Northern senior at CCNY said he "plans to go to Howard or Meharry Medical School. I feel touchy about being a Negro and being rejected. I would have a better chance of admission and social acceptance at a Negro college." A sophomore at the same college said that he "had a chance to go to Columbia on a partial scholarship but I turned it down because I thought the people would be above me socially." A Southern senior is going to "attend a Negro medical school so I am anticipating no difficulties."

A small number of these young men, in talking about the branch of the armed services that they prefer, if and when they must serve, made explicit mention of racial matters. However, we recall in this connection that the majority look forward to serving in the Air Force, a service which is known to offer the Negro good opportunities for advancement.

A Northern high-school senior stated: "The Navy still has prejudice but the Air Force is better in this respect." A Southern high-school senior who plans to enlist in the Air Force was motivated to do so because even a decade or more ago, his father had succeeded in getting a good assignment. Another who also plans to enlist remembered in passing: "I've never seen a Negro pilot and I wonder if there's a racial problem."

During the course of their interviews a few young men made sweeping generalizations about the role of race in their lives. A Southern sophomore remarked: "My life has been determined by the factor of race." A classmate commented: "What I will be doing in the future depends upon the condition of my race." One Southern senior said that he "has not been exposed to hard-core segregation, so I can't say what effect race will have on my future plans." Finally, we have this statement from a Southern senior: "Civil Rights is helping me carry out my plans. It's great to be a Negro today."

We find in these specific and general statements about the factor of race in the shaping of their lives a general downgrading of its influence. These young people recognize that, at the present moment in the nation's history, to be a Negro may result in as many advantages as disadvantages. They are not unduly disturbed when they recognize the disadvantages since most of them believe that they can surmount the difficulties with a little extra effort or tact. And since desegregation is opening many new opportunities to them, they understand that certain special opportunities will continue to be made available to Negroes. They will have preferences on the faculties of Negro colleges, they will have special roles in Civil Rights organizations, and the political leadership of a newly enrolled and voting minority will represent an important new presence.

Although they do not believe that American society will become completely "color blind," they assume that color is a factor of rapidly diminishing importance and that their future and particularly the future of their children will depend primarily on individual abilities and energies. Whether or not a Negro succeeds will increasingly depend on his qualities as a person, not as a Negro.

Their general views about the future and about the type of lives they envision for their children include reflections about matters of race, as well as about trends that are working to reshape the nation's economic and social life.

The following quotations demonstrate the ways in which these youths picture the world they will be living in as adults. A Northern sophomore said: "Education will probably cost more and there'll be an increasing emphasis on education. If trends continue, specialization will become more intense. With more people going to college, there'll be greater competition for jobs and careers."

Another Northern sophomore thinks: "By that time, college will probably be mandatory—it won't be a question of *whether* one wants to go. There might even be a law to this effect, since white America doesn't want to see the Russians or the Chinese take over, or even move ahead." A classmate said: "We now emphasize a Master's degree. In twenty years, it will be the Ph.D." Another remarked: "Being a Negro is a help now but probably won't be then, because people will have begun to see Negroes as people. It is possible there may be a reactive bias toward Negroes because of special treatment Negroes are receiving now. There will be greater competition, greater specialization, and the present character of professions may alter."

A Southern sophomore remarked: "The way the world is going, there may be no world in ten years. In some areas I know the world will be much better than in my father's time; in some ways, there will be the same ruts. Technologically it will have advanced but people will be so busily concerned about technological advances that they will tend to see other people as parts of the technology and not as human beings."

A Northern college senior thinks: "People will probably be uplifted because they will have had more success in achieving goals. There will be a reduction in hopelessness." Another in this same group feels: "Whites will always have fears and reservations about Negroes." A Northern college senior stated: "Education will be completely open but more expensive. Job opportunities will be greater but competition will be made intense. The well-rounded man will be a thing of the past. Values will be different because our society will be more mechanized and more specialized."

A Northern high-school boy said: "I expect things to be fantastic. Technologies will be improved, opportunities will be better, and so will earning facilities." A classmate thinks: "As the years go by the growing complexity of our society makes increasing demands educationally but the acquisition process seems to be easier for each generation." Another boy said: "I guess everyone will have to have an M.A. instead of a B.A."

Several points are suggested by the foregoing. These young men are not wildly optimistic. They see many important forces at work and they suspect that these powerful political, technological, and economic trends may swamp even the issue of race relations. They presume that if the world survives it will offer more opportunities to all people, including Negroes.

The way they see these broadened opportunities can be gauged by reviewing what they have to say about the lives that their children are likely to lead. They are overwhelmingly convinced that their children's lives will be better than theirs. A Southern sophomore said: "My opportunities are greater than my father's and my children's will be greater than mine." Similarly, a Northern

high-school senior believes: "My children will be better
off than I. It goes in a cycle." One of his classmates
hopes: "The situation will be even better for them than
it is for me and I think it's pretty good for me." Another
thinks: "Each generation would represent more improvement." A Southern high-school senior believes that
his children "will have a wonderful life." A fellow student looks forward to the time when "children can go as
high as the sky. If you are ambitious, no one can stop
you." Still another Atlanta high-school student expects:
"My children will have it better than my father or me.
So far they would say all of us are doing all right. Let's
keep it going down the line."

A few young men have some reservations about their
children's lives. A Northern sophomore, for example, remarked: "If the world is still around and if there are no
interfering difficulties such as outlook, deformity, illness,
or other such unpredictables, the situations will be very
good for them, except that the human problems will always be there." A Northern high-school senior thinks
that his children will be better off, "but by the time they
grow up there might be a population explosion and less
jobs." A Northern college senior feels "uncertain about
foreseeing what the situation will be like for my children. I tend to brood about the future."

Here are some comparisons they make between their
own circumstances and those they visualize for their
progeny. Some see the greatest difference in education.
"I am pretty sure my children will be obligated to go to

college whereas I'm choosing to go," said a Northern high-school senior. A Northern sophomore thinks: "It may take longer to get educated because of specialization needs and the need for a broadly based general education." These young men anticipate increased demands for their sons but do not imply that they cannot be met. Others look forward to increased educational opportunities. A Northern sophomore said: "Since I hope to be in a better economic state than my parents, I will be able to provide my children with better educational opportunities than my parents were able to make available to me." A Southern sophomore hopes: "Life for my children will be several levels above mine. They will probably be able to have a better education and a better foundation." A classmate remarked: "My children will be able to get jobs and educational opportunities more in line with their abilities." A Northern high-school senior believes: "My children will have more opportunities since there will be less segregation and better teaching."

A few boys discuss social differences. A Northern high-school senior expects that his offspring will "live in a better neighborhood. They will go to better schools and they will have more social activities." Another in this group said: "My children will have more luxuries and more leisure time for play and avocations." A Northern sophomore predicts "more socio-cultural participation. The Civil Rights movement will exalt feelings of pride and this will lead to more social involvement." A Northern sophomore who foresees "more educational specialization and increased competition" expects his children, nevertheless, "to be better off socially, economically, and psychologically."

With regard to the question of economic differences, a Northern college senior feels that his children "will have a much brighter childhood and future. I've received the culture but I don't have the finances. They will have both." A Northern sophomore said: "I expect to be better off financially than my parents and this will flow over into better advantages for my children than those I enjoyed." A classmate thinks: "There will be more money available. That may make it easier for my children to achieve but the achievement process may present greater difficulty. The computer age may bring about greater specialization and a greater need for planning."

Some spoke of generally broadened opportunities. A Southern sophomore said: "My generation has the problem of adjusting to the opportunities which have recently become available. I believe that my children won't have this problem because they will be regarded more as individuals and will have access to anything they want to pursue. When a person comes across something new they have to get adjusted, but my children would just regard it as life and living." A classmate said: "There will be a great difference in the life of my children. My parents had to accept jobs which did not challenge their ability. My children will be able to get jobs and educational opportunities more in line with their abilities." A Northern sophomore anticipates "greater opportunity than now due to more and newer fields opening up." A Northern college senior said: "If the trend of more privileges and opportunities continues, my children will be better able to realize their goals without major hindrance probably better than I have been able to."

Some of the boys described expected differences in family attitudes and influences. A Northern senior said: "There probably will be almost as big a difference as between my father and myself. My children will not have to create their intellectual atmosphere as I had to." A classmate thinks his children "will have a more meaningful father figure." Another Northern senior feels: "I have more sense than my parents in rearing children and I think they'll be better off. Also, I have a different outlook in life and my home will be a better home." Another youth in this group said: "They will be better off. I will be better equipped than my father was. Through my father's efforts I had it better than he did and through mine my children will have it better than I did." A Northern high-school senior anticipates: "Things will be as good or better than they were for me. For one thing, my children won't be a minister's son—they'll probably feel a bit freer than I did."

A small minority, who do not disagree with the optimism of their fellows, nevertheless warned about such matters as the greater competition that Negro youngsters will face once they participate more fully in a desegregated society. But this was a minor reservation.

Most parents look forward to realizing some of their unfulfilled goals through their children. Our young men were no exception. This is what they wish for their children and how they look forward to helping them realize the aspirations they had for them.

With regard to aspirations concerning education, a Northern college senior said: "I hope my children will get things I didn't get. I would love for them to go to college." A classmate said: "I would push my children in the direction of higher education because I believe that a good education is the necessary basis for any career." A Northern sophomore plans "to emphasize education and degrees. A B.A. will not be good enough twenty years from now." A Northern high-school senior would like to give his children "all the education they can absorb." A classmate wants his "sons to go through college and his daughters through high school." A Southern sophomore said: "My main objective will be to make life easier for my children. I would hope to be able to provide a good education for them without financial strain."

Although educational aspirations were most frequently mentioned, some youths verbalized other hopes for their children. A Southern college senior said: "I'd like my children to learn the basic values of life. I would like my children to have every advantage." A Southern sophomore wants his children "to understand their cultural heritage, to know that they have nothing to be ashamed of." A Northern college senior wants his children "to be involved in politics and law. These areas are critical be-

cause of their policy-determining nature." Another
Northern senior wants them "to be more aware of and
more involved in the black community. I would want
them to help change the white man's stereotype of a
Negro as a hustler and numbers runner." Still another
Northern senior said his children "will be taught how to
prosper in a white Protestant environment." A Northern
high-school senior wants his offspring to be professionals: "You are most secure and least dependent when you
work for yourself." A classmate would like one of his
children "to be a doctor, since I cannot be one, but it
would be up to them." And finally, a classmate expressed
a threefold dream that his children be "happy, aware,
and realistic."

How will they contribute to the realization of their aspirations for their children? Here are some of their comments. A Northern sophomore would like "to provide
the appropriate atmosphere and active interest" in the
achievement of his children's educations and career
plans. A classmate said: "My main hope would be to be
in a position to help them achieve in terms of their
wishes and aptitudes." Another said: "I would urge my
children to study. I can look back and see that I didn't
study as much as I should have. I think I wasted time
when I was a kid. I could have read more than I did. As a
parent, I would guide them. My parents guided me." A
Northern sophomore thinks that his "role will be to in-
still ideas and to help them achieve. My achievement
will be an example." Still another said: "With regard to

my children, I would try to be as unspecific as possible but stimulating. For example, my father approves of my becoming a lawyer but did not suggest it to me." A Northern high-school senior plans "to try to influence them to go to college but only if they want to. The only pressure I would put on them would be in regard to going to college."

A Southern high-school senior believes that "children should do something. I don't want to make it too easy for them. I'd let them help some even if only to the extent of their earning their own spending money." A classmate talked about his son: "I'd tell him, I'll pay your tuition through college and you pay your tuition through graduate school, but if he decided on graduate work I would help him."

A Southern college senior said: "I would provide unconditionally for their college and on the basis of their own achievements I would provide those that could go further with support. I don't think people should push, but if a child showed interest I would pay his way unconditionally." An opposite point of view was expressed by a classmate who said: "I believe I would send them through undergraduate school and assist them in graduate work as much as I could, but I would not assume the whole responsibility because I feel if you work hard you appreciate things when you get them."

Speaking of his children, a Southern sophomore said: "In their life they could have everything." A classmate remarked: "I am going to teach my children that they are black children, not white. I would try to teach them who they are by teaching them about their history and where they come from." A classmate wants his children to be "independent. I don't want them to get the idea that because their Daddy is rich that he will pay all their expenses. I do want them ready to accept, not worry about money, however." Another classmate said: "I would be willing to sacrifice anything for my children for them to have the best possible educations."

Northern college seniors reported their plans for their children. One remarked that he will "try to rear them to understand that it is through education that building for tomorrow becomes feasible." A few are able to contemplate the possibility that their children may be disinterested in or incapable of attending college. One thinks: "If my children were not interested in academic subjects, per se, I'd make sure they received a specialized education which would prepare them for a vocation." Another stated: "My role will be to present them with logical alternatives and to stimulate them to push harder in some directions." Another said: "I will try to give them emotional security without lavishing things on them. Adversity and obstacles help aspirations and motivations." Still another expected that his having "advanced degrees will probably stimulate and influence them to make a similar achievement. I would push my children in the direction of higher education because I believe that a good education is the necessary basis for any career."

Since our young men realize that fundamental

changes in race relations and in the position of the Negro in the United States cannot be achieved except over long periods of time, they understandably expect their children to reap some of these benefits. They know that their parents have traveled part of the way which has made it easier for them to start out. They look forward to giving their children even better starts; therefore, their children should be in good positions to enjoy all the benefits of a democratic and affluent United States.

In fact, some of these who talked most perceptively about the future were a little concerned that their children might have it too easy and thus be handicapped. A few are making plans to guard against such an eventuality. The politics of race relations has receded far into the background; its place has been taken by concern with the psychology of motivation!

These young men look forward to the substantial disappearance of segregation and discrimination during the lifetime of their children, but none touched upon the question of marriage between the races. They expect that areas of serious racial conflict will have been reduced and eliminated, but intermarriage is neither a conscious preoccupation nor a necessary concomitant of equal status.

This has been the history of many other minority groups who have succeeded in becoming integrated into American society. Race has played a small role in the lives of these young men so far; they expect it to play a smaller role during their adult years, and they anticipate that while it will be a factor in the lives of their children it will have minimal significance.

These young Negroes do not believe that the whites will lose all of their prejudice or that Negroes will live on terms of intimacy with the white population. Their optimism is more restrained. They look forward to a multi-racial democracy in which Negroes will not be inhibited from exercising either their rights or their talents. They look forward to equality with all other Americans who are able and willing to study, to work, and to shape their lives as they see fit. These young men want no more than this opportunity and they are quite sure that they will get it.

9: THE ROAD AHEAD

This study of the aspirations of middle-class Negro youth has sought to uncover the extent to which considerations of race continue to enter into their career plans. We hoped to learn the extent to which young men whose parents are able to encourage and support them are perceiving and responding to the developing opportunities for Negroes. Never far from the center of our interest was the question of whether recent changes in race relations are likely to enable the Negro minority to become integrated into white America in a manner similar to that followed by other ethnic groups. In other words, will education and economic status supersede race as the major determinant of the Negro's position in the larger community?

We found that these young men are making their plans for the future in terms of their interests and aptitudes, with little reference to their being Negro. Like middle-class white youths, these young people come from environments which predisposed them to pursue higher education to prepare for preferred positions in the labor market. Educational attainment, with its promise of occupational opportunity, is basic to their planning.

Since their racial identity has not heretofore interfered seriously with the shaping of their goals, they see little reason to anticipate future barriers because of this factor. They have already achieved an educational status superior to that of most Negroes—and even most whites—and they feel confident about their future.

But race is not totally absent from their thinking and planning. Few disregard it completely. They believe that the Civil Rights movement is largely responsible for the broadened opportunities for themselves and for other Negroes. Several suggest that since the Negro protest is succeeding primarily in such areas as public accommodations and college integration, activity on this front will have significance for them as members of the middle-class but will have little impact upon the lives of the Negro masses. However, they do not see the movement as the keystone of their personal futures. Time and again, they state that their prospects will depend upon their performance in school and on the job. Although they appreciate the new educational and career possibilities that are becoming available, they tend to consider these peripheral to their own efforts. Many state that the nature and extent of Civil Rights accomplishments are incidental to the realization of their goals. They see the major personal effect of the Civil Rights movement as general encouragement of their will to succeed.

Their awareness of and response to broadening opportunities do not blind them to the possibility that desegregation may mean increased competition for them. In the past, middle-class Negroes functioned almost exclusively within the Negro community, where their small number and comparative superiority made it relatively easy for the qualified to rise to positions of prominence. They realize that the relaxation of racial restrictions will provide them access to the larger society but will also place them in competition with larger numbers than earlier generations of Negroes had to face. Yet few consider this to be a major threat. Instead, they accept the challenge and expect to be able to meet it.

Because of their stress on personal accomplishment as the major route to achievement, many think that additional legislation will have limited effectiveness in speeding their future progress. Perhaps this is why a significant proportion of the total group have had only spectators' roles in the struggle for Civil Rights, and why many of the activists appear to be slowly disengaging. The dominant view is that their most effective contribution to advancing the future of the Negro is to assure their own success. They see themselves in the same relation to the Negro lower classes as that of middle-class whites to poor whites. They deplore the conditions of the Negro poor and look forward to making some contribution toward alleviating their misfortunes, but, except for the few who plan careers in community work, their goals are directed toward improving their own circumstances.

Most of the Negro leadership of the Civil Rights movement has come from the middle class. However, leaders are exceptional by definition, and only a very few young men in our study expect to play such a role as their life's work. While many are willing to run risks in the protest movement, they are not angry young men. For the most part, their childhoods were sufficiently protected so that instead of distrusting the white community, they look forward to closer associations in school, on the job, and as neighbors. Yet, although they expect greater social integration, they do not deliberately seek assimilation through intermarriage. They do not necessarily reject such a possibility, but at this time it is not part of the equality to which they aspire.

Despite the widespread belief that the attitudes of the educated Negro have been influenced by the emergence of independent nations in Africa, there was little evidence of this in our study. Whether or not they are aware that the changes in American racial relations might be partly ascribed to the impact of African nationalism, we doubt that these young men would find this relevant to their own concerns. It is evident that their roots are deep in the American experience; in fact most of the Southerners look forward to continuing to live in the South. Although the South has been especially hostile and oppressive toward the Negro, times are changing and most Southern Negroes feel at home there. This may reflect the success which middle-class Negroes have achieved in certain parts of the South, particularly in Atlanta, in special enclosures where they are able to lead dignified, if somewhat constricted, lives.

Although most of them aspire to places in an integrated society, many of them attend or plan to attend Negro colleges. This may be because less rigid entrance requirements permit the admission of Southern boys with inferior preparation. When integrated preparatory schooling becomes more generally available in the South, it is probable that many more Negro students will be able to enter predominantly white institutions. However, it is not only their educational inadequacies which dictate their choice of Negro colleges; propinquity, sentiment, and racial self-consciousness also play parts. Nevertheless, broadening educational opportunities are such that present and prospective students at Negro colleges contemplating further education look forward to entering integrated graduate schools.

Many know that attending segregated schools and living in segregated communities means that they are cut off from valuable experiences. There is much about the white world in which they expect to make their way that is strange and alien to them. Since a large number of these young Negro men come from outside of the white community, they do need special guidance and counseling. Yet, it is difficult for them to obtain and assess the information they need. This is a significant barrier to their full exploitation of new opportunities. While some recognize and regret this lack of information, others are not fully aware of its importance since they attend segregated schools where they compete only with Negroes, and this interferes with the development of realistic evaluations of their own talents and capacities.

Despite their racial handicap, these young people had sufficiently good starts so that they believe that they can shape the kinds of lives they desire to lead. With college or graduate degrees they will have access to good jobs, jobs that will yield them sufficient income and security upon which to build. They look forward to doing work that not only will pay well but will provide them with personal satisfaction and fulfillment. They look forward to marrying and to having children they will be able to propel toward still higher achievements.

Some believe that, on balance, it is an advantage to be a Negro at the present stage of the country's history when society is finally attempting to make amends. The turning point has been reached and passed. Race is receding as a barrier to participation in the larger society. Equality of opportunity is finally changing from a promise into a reality for many Negroes.

Although we have no way of knowing the degree to which these young mens' goals will be realized, it appears likely that their expectations, for the most part, are realistic. Some of the younger boys have not completely abandoned their childhood fantasies, but most of the students appear to have made rational choices in terms of their own aptitudes and interests and are assessing realistically the external forces with which they will have to contend. Thus, their statements of intention serve not only as indicators of the way they wish to proceed, but also of the general direction in which they actually will proceed.

To what extent can these findings be applied to other middle-income Negro youth and to young Negroes from less favorable backgrounds?

There is every reason to believe that, despite its small size and its limited geographical representation, this group is illustrative of urban middle-class Negro youth. The minimal criteria for selection disclosed disparities of background and experience which fall within the range of the middle class. But these individual differences did not significantly influence the outlook of these youths. Almost without exception, they have positive responses to America's new open-door policy and exhibit confidence in their ability to succeed in the larger society.

Since knowledge of the broadened opportunities for Negroes is spreading rapidly, there is reason to believe that other youths from middle-class families are also aiming high. We know that high socio-economic status engenders high aspirations, but the aspirations of Negroes, regardless of status, has long been constricted because of their exclusion from the world beyond the ghetto. The youths in this study expect to move into this world, to pursue a broader range of career choices, and to perform in a wider arena. Their confidence in this regard suggests that they are speaking not only for themselves but for others like themselves.

Findings about Negroes from middle-class families cannot be directly applied to those from lower-class homes. Few who grow up in poverty and deprivation aim high since they see no prospect of accomplishing high goals. They do not have the support necessary for achievement: family stability, economic security, and educational advantages. Regardless of race, without these prerequisites for achievement children are unlikely to progress much beyond the level of their parents. The chances for poor Negroes are even less since they must also contend with the disabilities of color.

The families of the young men whom we have studied have succeeded in escaping the poverty and deprivation which continue to hold most Negroes prisoner. But their number is relatively small because the intensity of the deprivation and discrimination with which Negroes have had to contend for so long had prevented many of them from escaping from their impoverished circumstances. To assert that, because a minority of Negroes have been able to achieve varying degrees of success, it is now within the capabilities of all Negroes to advance, is to ignore the realities of lower-class Negro life which inhibit initiative and enterprise.

It is unrealistic to expect young Negroes who do not know their fathers, whose mothers can barely feed and clothe them, who live amidst vice and corruption, who attend poor schools, to aim high and to acquire sufficient drive and competence to enable them to escape from the poverty into which they were born and bred. This is especially so today when educational preparation is an increasingly important determinant of occupation and income. At the same time, the proportion of jobs available to the unskilled has shrunk. The child who fails in school casts a shadow of adult failure.

Until recently, both Negro and white leadership assumed that when the Negro finally acquired his political rights, there would no longer be a need for social intervention. But this expectation has been proved wrong. The wide diffusion of this theory has complicated matters, however, since many whites believe that the Negro problems which remain can be solved by passing a few more laws; and many Negroes react with increasing frustration to the fact that Civil Rights legislation has failed to improve their lives.

We do not discount the contribution of the Civil Rights movement during the past decade; nevertheless, justice in the courtroom and access to the ballot box will not enable the mass of Negroes to participate fully in American life. Political equality is only one of the necessary conditions which will enable Negroes to enjoy the promises of an affluent America.

Unless we make a broad and continuing commitment to use all the instruments of society—government, the private sector, and the Negro community itself—to change the conditions and circumstances of the socially disorganized, impoverished, and poorly educated Negroes, the gap between the seriously disadvantaged Negroes and the more affluent middle class, Negro and white, may widen. Such an eventuality can bring in its wake only greater tensions, frustrations, and hostility.

While the white community must create the avenues of escape for more and more young people who today are still locked up in the ghetto, the Negro middle class has a key part to play. In the past, knowing that it could accomplish little and that it might jeopardize its own hard-won gains, it has largely ignored the problem. But the situation has begun to change. More and more Negroes have succeeded in excaping from poverty; the white community is more willing to take affirmative action; and the Civil Rights movement has contributed markedly to raising the aspirations of the Negro masses.

Improvement in the material well-being of those who live in poverty and suffer its afflictions is, of course, a requirement of the first order, and efforts being made toward this end should certainly be continued and strengthened. This is a moral imperative for an affluent society. But merely to provide the necessities of everyday living will not enable the Negro to escape from his trap. Entrance into the middle class depends primarily on individual performance. Only access to good education and good training can provide access to the higher level occupations which determine middle-class status and fuller participation in American life.

The Civil Rights movement had done much to lay bare the structure and functioning of American society, white and Negro. With respect to the Negro community, it has revealed serious inadequacies in social organization and in leadership potential. These defects will not be quickly remedied. Optimism that the racial problem in the United States will be successfully resolved is founded upon the sizable minority of Negroes who are able to graduate from college and to find good positions in the economy. The college graduates who enter government service, business, and the professional world anticipate making their way in a white world, and there is every reason to expect them to succeed.

Middle-class Negro youths are in a good position to take advantage of the new opportunities that white America at long last has begun to make available to them. Not so, the Negro poor. Much more must be done to help them reach the qualifying line so that they too can enter the mainstream. Middle-class Americans, whites and Negroes alike, have an obligation to help turn the promise of equality of opportunity into a reality for all the poor. No democracy can afford to make specious promises.

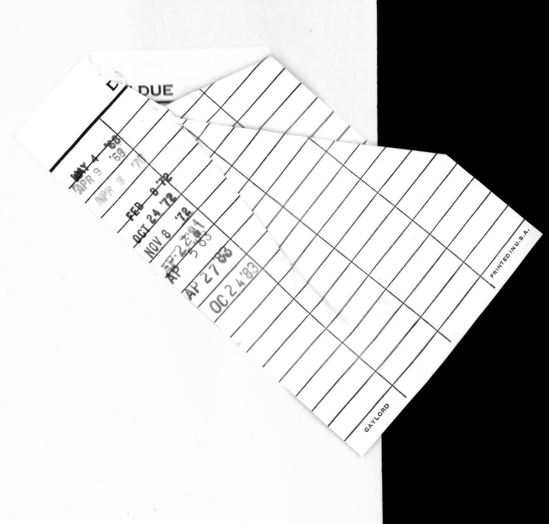